HA! HA!

HA! HA!

RÉJEAN DUCHARME

Translated by David Homel

TORONTO
Exile Edition
1986

This edition is published by Exile Editions Ltd.,
69 Sullivan Street, Toronto, Canada

Sales Distribution
General Publishing Co. Ltd.
30 Lesmill Road, Don Mills, Ontario M3B 2T6

Typset in STEMPEL GARAMOND by TUMAX TYPESETTING CO., LTD.
Designed by LOU LUCIANI
ISBN 0-920428-35-5

HA! HA!

PART ONE

Set:

A big apartment, furnished in Furniture Warehouse style. An expensive violet shag rug. A gigantic Tiffany-style lamp, something from Lighting Unlimited.

The door is at the back, squarely in the middle. Stage right: the kitchen that leads into the diningroom, and the bathroom door.

Stage left: the two bedroom doors, one next to the other. Center stage, facing the audience like a television set: the livingroom. Roger's king-sized sofa and tilt-back Lazy-Boy armchair dominate the scene. Between the two: a Sputnik-style stereo with a built-in record player and tape recorder. On the other side of the armchair: a stand-up ashtray topped by little lights that slowly blink on and off at equal intervals.

Characters:

SOPHIE: Impassioned. Complicated. A lot of freedom and color in her dress but not much "taste." Long and thin, a red-head. In her thirties.

ROGER: Sophie's lover. Dressed the way the apartment is decorated. With a handsome moiré bathrobe and two fine furry slippers. Porcine and pale. A prince-of-poets attitude, a leave-me-alone-don't-bother-me attitude. No special language. Speaks well, speaks poorly. Speaks slang, English, Spanish, pig Latin. Awesome, then childish. Flames up and flickers out like the crown of his ashtray. Chomps on a cigar that does not seem to belong in his face: he has such trouble smoking it. Rings on too many fingers. In his forties.

MIMI: Bernard's wife. Very young compared to the others. Pretty much their antithesis: round, passive and reserved in her dress. Sickly sensitivity in mind and body. She prefers a hat and gloves.

BERNARD: Handsome, well dressed. Intelligent, corrupt, end-of-the-line alcoholic. From his father he inherited a garage and an apartment block where Sophie and Roger live, filling in as superintendents. Has given up believing in his inheritance. Apparently still believes in the sentiments he has concocted for Sophie, his boyhood friend.

Music:
Michel Pagliaro's *Ti-Bidon.*

SCENE I

$$\boxed{}$$

(Roger, Sophie)

The click-click of a tape recorder, the squeal of a tape rewinding. Lights up. Roger begins recording his "Brittle Speech." He reads from a wrinkled scrap of paper, holding his nose.

ROGER: Brittle speech from the four-legged drone, two of which are weak in the knees: "The new biodegrading strength of Rictus Power with improved enzymes stirs up the murky colors of the Saint Florid, the river that squirts like a skunk." *(He plays back the recording, happy with himself as he listens.)* Infectious! ... Abjectionable! ... Hopeless! ... Repugnant! ... Izza wonderful! Izza delightful!

> *Noise at the door. Roger turns off the machine and sinks back into his armchair, cigar in mouth. Sophie enters, puts down her shopping bag on the kitchen table. Goes and kisses Roger.*

SOPHIE: So?

ROGER: So what?

SOPHIE, *taking offense immediately*: What's eating you ... again? I didn't say olé, I didn't say splattering bladders or big fat hen ... I just said so! So? ... So? ... Get up on the wrong side again? So? What time was it? ... Four o'clock? Four-thirty? Five? ... Spend an hour in the bathroom and it bored you to death! So? ... So? ...

ROGER: Hang up, the line's busy!

SOPHIE: Come again?

ROGER: Ease up, I'm telling you! I'm developing my thoughts and your nitrates are ruining my dyes. You're zig, you're zag, you're negative: put it in gear, take off, show us your dust. Hustle your buns, shake a leg, get cooking, toots, your stew's on fire, rattle your bones, show us your lark.

SOPHIE: Now that's the living end! ... Now that's the limit!

ROGER, *forming a trumpet around his ear*: Permiso? ...

SOPHIE, *louder*: You're just hoping I don't have the guts to throw you out! Just keep hoping!

ROGER, *holding his nose*: You put me in such a state ... You exacerbate my apathy. Do it summore, do it encore.

SOPHIE, *going to the refrigerator to calm down*: Who's looking for trouble here? I come back from work, I give you a kiss, I'm all peppy ... is that an excuse to get pissed off? What did I do to you?

ROGER: It's not the little you did, it's what you didn't. You have a bubbly personality, you think it's something to be proud of, but instead of bubbling over quietly in a corner, mixing and matching while I'm relaxing, you broach me, you approach me!

SOPHIE, *throwing the groceries into the fridge*: You treat me like a scouring pad, a dishrag!

ROGER: Happy?

SOPHIE: Overjoyed!

ROGER: If you're happy, then wiggle and wriggle and squirm! Throw ourself on the ground and squeal!

SOPHIE, *throwing herself on the ground and squealing*: You asked for it!

ROGER, *ironically during Sophie's little song and dance, which isn't so little after all*: Makes you feel yourself again, doesn't it? (...) Casts the devil out, whatcha say? (...) Oh wow! Holy shit! What kind of fuel you burning? (...) Watch out! Beware! Aware! Don't strip your gears! Don't dent your body ... Hell doesn't quit at five-thirty ... Imagine what you'll be like at seven ... all out of gas. You won't be running hard at seven-thirty or eight ... with your radials going flop-flop-flop!

SOPHIE, *too much wriggling, too much squealing, out of breath*: That enough?

ROGER: With a good head of steam like you had, I wouldn't have stopped ... Turn over, sputter, bust your muffler, sizzle ... Sugar bushes, styrofoam poles, sweetlights: crash head-on, have a terrible accident, get critically injured, live intensely! Peel them spuds, articulate, dust yourself off, you coagulate when you stop! ...

SOPHIE, *all stretched out on the floor, spirits calmed, lascivious now*: Why don't you dust me of instead? You've got a bigger head than I do ...

ROGER: Hustle your buns! Make an effort! Escape your mucilaginous destiny if you can!

SOPHIE: That's right ... Tell me to manipulate myself. Tell me to motivate myself, that's all I know how to do ... Talk! Talk to me! Let's babble! Not the most nutritious sustenance ... but it's all I got in the fridge till my next paycheck ...

ROGER, *smoking, watching the smoke rise toward the ceiling*: You're gonna shtop if you resht shtretshed out ... Berfumes on the wind bravel, they banish into the air ... but the wee breeze breezes them. Stir yourself! ... Otherwise curl up in your formaldehyde and screw on your top on the double.

SOPHIE, *obscenely*: Come quick, screw on my top till it squeaks. Come, lover, apply your theories all over me ... Let me have something on credit, tomorrow's payday ...

ROGER: That's right, you fish, wiggle your fins!

SOPHIE, *on four legs, her behind in the air*: Give me a love pat ... I'm your spoiled little brat and I need a good spanking ... You're right, you know, of all of us, I'm the worst off, I'm the only woman here who doesn't know what to do with her body. Shock me, squall me, strike me. Make something out of my body.

ROGER: That's right, Elsie, squirt your milk! Pull out the stops! Point, sniff, trot; dig, scratch, ferret! ... Send the earth flying with your hind legs!

SOPHIE: You've flopped so far into that thing, you'll never get back up again! I bet you've got a little something hidden in there, but don't worry, I won't sink that low! (...) Grrrr!

ROGER, *rocking in his Lazy Boy, nodding his head*: Oodums! Oodums Poodums! Poodums oodums! ... Say it ain't so! ... Say it ain't so that that ...thathatha ... that after all this excavating in my stinking cavity with your cutexed nail ... thathatha ... that you're going to throw in the trowel and hang up your snakes! Oodums! Oodums poodums! Don't bitch at me, don't say I'm not your favorite bone no more, don't say you won't bury me sss sss so's I'll ripen and my marrow come sweating through my interstices!

SOPHIE, *standing up, hiking up her skirt, declaiming – like in the advertisement for Whisper pantyhose*: Whisper ...

ROGER: Watch your tush! I'm about to fake dragonian measures ... Glisten up ... Oodums poodums! *(Holding his nose)* I have no desire to awake with no desire! ... dragging my bag of bones like a soiled tablecloth after a surprise party! ...Scraping together my nerve from the bottom of the sink like a viscous fold of cold noodles!...

SOPHIE, *tears in her laughter*: Have you got a way with words! Ha! I'd like to compete but you laugh me off my feet, let me put in a word, you're no ordinary bird, hee hee ha ha. *(She holds her nose like Roger when he commits verbal delirium)* Yhourra strhange bhird! *(Laughs again)* Ha! ... Hahahahahaha! *(The absurdity of the situation bends her double)*

ROGER, *apocalyptic, more rocking and nodding*: First porno, now soap! The declining scale of chaos! You slay me! That's the ticket, wicket! Mush, mush, mush too mush!

SCENE 2

$$\boxed{}$$

(Roger, Bernard's voice, Sophie)

Blackout. Silence. The telephone rings and rings.

SOPHIE, *at the top of her lungs*: I'm on the can! Would your jaw break if you answered the phone just this once?

> *Lights on. Half-naked, Roger comes tearing out of his room at the back.*

ROGER, *on the telephone*: Hello, Fuller bushman!

BERNARD'S VOICE, *drunk, greasy, uproarious*: Hello, zat you, Sophie? Zat you, puss puss pussycat? ... scratch my back and lick my face ... Whoops ... (*The sound of the receiver falling from his hands*) Whoa now ... Whoa ... Get back here ... Hello hello?

ROGER, *louder and louder*: Yeah? That you, frou-frou? Chew your gum if you must but I can't understand a thing when you talk through your bubbles ...

BERNARD'S VOICE, *achingly tender*: In your arms, my Sophie, I'll come with no harm ... Isn't that beautiful? I was at the Place des Arts the other day, and I pictured myself in that Serge Lama song: (*Singing*) "I'm dirty without you, I'm disgusting without you ..." Isn't that just a beautiful compliment? ... (...) Put the good old days back on the fire, I'm coming home ... Not right now immediately ... my legs are a little too rubbery for that ... (*He sputters, he splatters.*)

ROGER: Listen, Fuller bushman, no offense, but there's a rub. You're barking in the wrong pond ... (*Holding his nose*) You're fishing up the wrong tree ... (*Lets go of his nose*) My name's Terry Berry, not Mary Perry!

BERNARD'S VOICE, *while Roger gets a cigar, lights up, smokes*: Ah, it's you, Master! ...Berni-ni-ni on the line ... What are you doing up at this hour ... you wet blanket you? Did you swing shifts or are you into frightening people full-time now? ...Anyway, I don't want to talk to you, I want Sophie ... and not just any Sophie ... not yours ... not the big stringbean ... Give me the pint-sized one, give me Cupcakes, who never had a bike and used to holler every time I rode past on mine, "Hey, Tunny-Fish, let me see your bike, will you?" I've got news for her: my pants leg is still tangled up in my chain. Tell her I'm on my way, but if she wants me she'll have to untwist me from around my fork ... *(He sputters and spatters.)*

ROGER, *as Sophie comes out of the bathroom, putting out her joint nervously*: Listen, frou-frou, the rub's gone but it's taken a turn for the worse, there's a bone now. A bone with two humps. Otherwise known as a dumb-bell ...

SOPHIE, *struggling with Roger to keep him from hanging up ... while Bernard is stricken with a violent fit of coughing exacerbated by emotional sobbing*: Let go! Let go, I'm telling you! ... Let go! Give it to me! If you don't give it to me, I'm warning you, I'll bite you, hard, hard! ...

BERNARD'S VOICE: Sophie? ... So ... Roger? Master? Master? Let me talk to my Cupcakes a minute, just a teensy-weensy minute, just sixty little seconds ...

SOPHIE, *managing to grab hold of the receiver*: Hello?

BERNARD'S VOICE, *bursting with joy*: Cupcakes ...

SOPHIE, *as Roger cuts them off*: Bernard! Where are you? Do you need anything? Are you in jail? ...

ROGER, *angrily returning to his room with the noise of the cut-off conversation growing on the soundtrack*: I'm warning you, you and your "I'm-on-the-can's" and your "Would-your-jaw-break-if-you-answered-just-this-once's?!"

SOPHIE, *having lit her joint again, exhaling a good long toke*: You're warning me, are you? *I'm* going to warn *you* ...

SCENE 3

(Sophie, Roger)

Blackout. The sound of the cut-off conversation continues and fades. Sophie turns on the radio. The sound of stations being changed. "My pantyhose put my lard on the line ... Whisper!"

SOPHIE, _echoing_: Whisper!

> _Changing stations again. Tuning in on "Ti-Bidon." Volume up. Lights. Sophie sings along with Michel Pagliaro. Dancing and doing the dishes. While Roger finishes balling up a few clippings from the Journal de Montréal whose corpse sprawls at the foot of the Lazy-Boy._

SOPHIE, _letting herself go, it's fiesta time_: Come on and dance — You sure didn't come here to make romance — Come on and dance — Don't stand there like a flea on a dog — Get up and do the frog ...

ROGER, _turning off the radio_: I thought you had one foot in the grave. How now, Lazarus? ... _(He gets up, moves his hips a little, imitating Sophie, sits down again)_ Whaddaya call that? The bigamist twist? And here I thought the nine-to-five in the salt mines had totally unraveled you ... Well? Well? Have you raveled yourself up again? _(...)_ _(...)_ Have they worked it out in Watts and Berkeley, is it smiles all around in Lebanon, everything's looking up in Rhodesia, have the wounds of Viet Man stopped attracting flies! The juice stopped squirting, the pus ebbed, the lips of the blood-red sea parted and Begin doesn't even get his feet wet as he marches to Pretoria! ... Well? Well? ... _(He gets up and does his little twist again.)_ Everything's falling to dust and you you yoyoyo you're strutting your stuff! ...

SOPHIE, _lovingly_: So what if my behavior is atrocious? It's not my fault if I feel like dancing. It's all those little swimmers you put inside. _(She rubs her belly.)_ They're still tickling me. _(She moves toward him, takes his face in her hands.)_ You're so fine ... What's on your mind? Nothing good between the lines?

ROGER, *one by one, throws the balled-up paper*: The Expos! ... (...) The Alouettes! (...) Drapeau! (...) Taillibert settling for fourteen instead of forty million! (...) The Princesse of Anne and her mare Flin-Flan who threw her off her back with nary a smack!

SOPHIE: You're right, how can anyone escape into those games, when you think of the ones in Mexico City ... three hundred students steeping in their own blood ...

ROGER: Who do you think I am anyway? You flutterfly around here all day, all afternoon you're fussing over the buffet and the frigid air and the killvinator and the garborator ... and all of the sudden pity fills your heart! Well? Well? Little Miss Flytail? *(He does his twist again)* Was the Garden of Gethsemane a coffee break? ... A piece of cake? ...

SOPHIE, *just as loving*: What is it you want? Whatever it is I've got it, I defy you to ask for something I don't have. I gave everything away to other men before I met you, but it was like they gave me back twice as much, to give to you ... Do you want it? What *do* you want? I'm here, overflowing, serve yourself ... *(She takes one of his hands)* Touch, feel my heart, feel how it fills my breast, I hardly have room to breathe. I'm alive, I'm made out of life. Touch, touch, feel how much I want to feel good ...

ROGER: Sure! Smoke another joint, you'll feel good ... What are you waiting for? Go hide in the toilet, go suck on your lollipop, go puff yourself up on smoke! Gwon, gwon! ...

SOPHIE, *an effort to keep calm*: I'm sick of fighting, Roger ... sick sick sick. I don't have the strength for it! ... (...) It's not my fault if I'm the easiest girl in the world to please. I've had all kinds of men and I've always managed to feel good. I've been with children and old men; nice guys and bastards; ignoramuses and know-it-alls; atomic bombs and wet firecrackers ... With you, no way. You're not interested. It disgusts you!

ROGER, *calmly*: When you chose me, you knew of my rebellion, you felt its enormity and you took pleasure in it ...

SOPHIE: I laughed. I thought it was all a joke!

ROGER: When you took me in this house, you signed a pact. You're bound until I unbind you. You gave me a mandate and I'm going to make you respect it. I'll keep filling it until one of us has completely demoralized the other, till each becomes the other through a kind of contagion, until I feel the first tremors of a truly volcanic eruption ... a possible potential maturely swelled with fissures and continental collapses.

SOPHIE, *overwhelmed, undone by these words*: I remember why *I* took *you*, as you put it! You were trembling like a leaf, bawling your eyes out, you were afraid of everything: your shadow, the police, the Gestapo! And your wife — she was your scariest bogeyperson! You were afraid to leave the Sportsman's Bar, afraid she was waiting on the other side of the door to disembowel you! I took you because I believed you. If I hadn't believed you I would have taken you anyway, the way I've taken plenty of others! ... Just for phun!

ROGER, *still calm, but beginning to rock back and forth*: Antagonized? Outraged? Violated? *(Sophie emits a cry of anger)* Too late, the debate is closed. The wha wha wha way things are now, I can't picture myself at the Sportsman's Bar hanging out with the hangers-on and ending up between another pair of grey sheets ...

SOPHIE, *circling around the Lazy-Boy, holding her belly*: Stop it! ... Stop! It's stopped being a game. (...) If you really hate me, hit me, that would be better. Break my arm, do something!

ROGER, *rocking more rapidly, his head beginning to nod*: Don't you wish! ... Oodums poodums! Poodums oodums!

SOPHIE, *increasing the dramatic tenor of her distress*: You're killing me, Roger! Sometimes I pretend to keep it from showing ... but it hurts too much, you're killing me ... You don't even believe me when I say how much you frighten me.

ROGER: The wha wha wha way things are now, we've stopped scoring the fears ... you should know that, oodums poodums — it's who's sunk deepest that counts, poodums oodums ...

SOPHIE, *bent double, as in childbirth*: Oh! ... Oh! ... My insides are all frozen, frost coats my veins ... *(Starting to moan)* I've got a hurt, Roger! I've got a hurt, right here, everywhere, in my belly ... I think

I'm going to have your baby, Roge, a big icy baby ... I'm going to have a snowman ...

ROGER: Oodums poodums ... Oodums poodums poodums oodums poodums ... Oodums oodums poodums oodums ...

SOPHIE, *struggling to keep her calm*: I'll make a deal with you, okay? We'll stay together, but we'll be apart, we'll each have our own space ... We won't say anything to each other, we won't do anything to each other, good or bad ... I want peace and quiet, you want peace and quiet, everybody wants peace and quiet ... all right? Okay? ... Let's start right now ... all right? All right? *(She rocks him gently.)* Answer me, please!

ROGER: First anarchy, then question period! After hysteria — terror, the Inquisition! Are you going to cut me some slack so I can relax? *(Sophie continues stifling her anger, she goes back to the kitchen sink.)* Huh? Huh? Huh? Huh? Huh? *(A five-second respite, then the telephone begins ringing off the hook.)* Great! Great! Great! Great! Asshold Finance calling! Everybody under the big top! (...) What did you do with the monthly payment? You had it; I counted it out for you! You didn't put it in the bank did you? Whadja do ... knowing you ... You went back for another helping at the Sportsman's Bar. You went to put another notch on your rusty old gun and the thing blew up in your face ... Zat it? Don't you think you've made me insecure enough as it is?

SOPHIE, *doing the dishes*: You're rambling again ... Who do you think is going to call us after six besides Bernard and Mimi? ... Unless you went and gave your number to your wife ... (...) I wouldn't blame you, mind you ... we're pretty boring together, the both of us ...

ROGER: Your little bloodsuckers wouldn't call. They don't need you to tell them you're broke ... They should know, they cut your pockets ...

SOPHIE, *going to answer the phone*: If it's Mimi, do you want to talk to her?

> *The telephone stops ringing. Sophie goes back to her chores.*

ROGER: If it's Mimi, let me talk to her. I've got news for her ... about my bitch's whelp. I raised the thing up: I taught him to ask to go out when he had to go ... he could recite poems ... and even ... pronounce four-legged brittle speeches from the drone ... (...) If your Bernard's on the line, he's finished, you can keep him!

SOPHIE: Great! Great! ... My Bernard's on the carpet now! ... I suppose *that* Bernard belongs to me! Because it wasn't you, right, it was me who asked him to hire you on as super in exchange for the apartment! Because it was me, it wasn't you who didn't have the strength to run the mop over the floors once a week, empty the incinerator when the ashes came spilling out and unlock the door for the tenants who forget their keys! Because the kind of Bernard you'd have wouldn't be such a sucker: he would have hired another super without a word when he realized you like sitting on your fat ass too much to get up and work! (...) You're posh, all right, you're refined! Don't I know it! You'd rather do without friendship than have to choose between four billion first-comers!

ROGER: You got it! You got the ticket ... wicket! *(He chortles)* We're screwed too tight tototo to live without it. *(He chortles)* Either that or we're too detached. *(Chortling)*

SOPHIE: Too plucked to the skin ...

ROGER, *playing along*: Too skinned to the raw, thenthenthen then we regret it! *(The giggle he had been trying to stifle bursts forth.)*

SOPHIE: I got you, you got me — we get each other!

ROGER, *trying to keep from laughing*: And the worst part is — I'm having the time of my life! (...) It's not enough to play the clone, I've got to do it all alone! *(He slaps himself in the face to call himself to order.)* Hey Sundown ... where'd you leave your dusky gown? *(Tragically)* Oh unkind Fate, I'll do your bidding, now that I've lost my sitting! ... *(Sophie waves her washrag to signal her presence.)* Sundown, your gown is in the lostnfound: it's gown and it won't be coming back! Ah, shit and midden, wave byebye and dry your eye, I'm shellacked, I'm varnished in my tracks!

SOPHIE: Yoo-hoo, I'm still here.

ROGER: Hang on tight! Getting seasick? Ready to lose your lunch? Don't let go! Don't try and get off before the ride's over, you'll hurt yourself! Don't worry, the last few miles of the shitstream are the rockiest! Oodums poodums poodums oodums! Martyrs are my meat!

SOPHIE, *coming to kneel at the foot of Roger's armchair, begging him softly*: Please, that's enough, love. We're far enough apart as it is. If we keep on like this we won't be able to turn back.

ROGER, *rocking, nodding, disassociated from reality*: Oodums oodums poodums! ... Poodums oodums oodums poodums poodums! ... Poodums poodums! ... Oodums! Poodums! Poodums!

SOPHIE, *stroking him, caressing him*: Shhhhhh ... That's enough. If you say Oodums poodums poodums oodums one more time, you'll have said it too much, it'll take over, like a disease. (...) (...) *(Roger continues muttering like a madman)* Shhhh ... Shh. I finished the dishes, I'm going to vacuum now ... *(She gets up)* Okay?

ROGER, *grabbing her violently by the arm*: Stay here! Stay right here! I abhor the vacuum!

SOPHIE, *docilely, getting on her knees again, stroking Roger's legs*: Okay ... Okay ...

ROGER: And start rubbing! Rub me for all you're worth! Go to it, cootie, scratch me till I bleed! ... Rub your dirty laundry in private, rub your own backyard, rub and scrub, fishwashers and vestal deadpan dishpan virgins! Rub and scrub, fluid in the lungs, droopy buns, major operations, unsightly facial hair, baggy grey crotchrags! Caress me! I'll even authorize a kiss ... but I like mine good and wet, so make sure you drag your face on the pavement first!

SOPHIE, *burying her tear-stained face in Roger's lap*: Oh yes ... Oh yes, my big meatloaf, oh yes!

ROGER: Rub me encore! Rub me summore! Give me a rash, give me pimples, give me teenage acne blemishes. I'll sop up the rest of your compassion ... but when it comes to your cankers ... no way José! ... You can keep your ulcers and your syruposis of the lover! Fuddle-duddle! Don't ask me to sit down at that Lord's Table. (...) (...) *(Asking Sophie comically)* How does that work as a brittle speech from the drone?

SOPHIE: It's wonderful! Wonderful!

ROGER, *applauding himself*: Then let's give it a hand!

SOPHIE, *applauding, getting to her feet, arms in the air*: Whooppee cushion! Bravo! Zorrrrro! Geronimo! Doug Riseborough! Lafleur skating up-ice on thin air, the wind in his hair — Wham! King Kong Korrab clips his wings! Pass it to Steve Shot with his big slapshutt, a bullet in the butt! Let her rip! Put it in! You'll be the king of the angels! THE KING OF LOS ANGELES!

ROGER, *catching her, making her kneel again*: Sit down and hand me that thing! Who're you trying to suck in with your vacuum, me? Me in your arms, your shadeless palms, your endless impasse, me in your deadend Eden?

SOPHIE: Yes!

> *(Applause from Sophie, but more timid this time. She does not know what to expect from Roger, who reflects on her latest declarations.)*

ROGER: Might as well ... Why not? Something within me finds delectation ...

SOPHIE, *interrupting him*: Oh yes!

ROGER: Repuke, repute, repeat after me ... and after Stanislaw Ignacy Witkiewicz *(Holding his nose)*: "Something within me finds delectation in this endless sacrifice into bottomless mediocrity ..."

SOPHIE, *repeating, in the same tone, with nose held. The lights go down, except for a spot on her*: "Something within me finds delectation in this endless sacrifice into bottomless mediocrity ..."

ROGER, *triumphant (Black out)*: Whisper!

SCENE 4

```
┌──────────                              ──────────┐
│                                                  │
│                                                  │
└──────────                              ──────────┘
```

(Mimi's voice, Sophie, Bernard)

Sophie dialing the phone. Ringing is heard from the other end of the line. Lights. Sophie is alone, nervous, smoking a joint.

MIMI'S VOICE, *breathless, panicked*: Hello! Hello! Hello!

SOPHIE: Hello Mimi listen I've got to see you! I'm in trouble over my head you've got to help me I'm afraid come over right away.

MIMI'S VOICE, *disappointed, tension dropping off, in her martyr voice*: Oh, it's you ... Let me tell you, you're knocking at the wrong door, I'm in worse shape than you are. If you've seen Bernard, tell me, please. He hasn't been home for two nights, we've been looking for him everywhere for three days. There's something terribly wrong ... he's lost touch ... I'm afraid he's gone unhinged ... I'm gonna want to go crazy.

SOPHIE, *cooled by Mimi's tone; sighs then turns ironic*: He's gone on a drunk ... so what? He pulls that one on you every week. You married him like that. So what?

MIMI'S VOICE: He left with the car!

SOPHIE: What do you mean "he left with the car"? ... Are you jealous of the car now?

MIMI'S VOICE, *wounded*: You're so horrid! ... Is that why you called up, to hurt me again? ... And besides *(Sobbing)*, if you don't mind me mentioning it ... Bernard had "stoppped," and you started him up again!

SOPHIE: What are you talking about? I've never had a drink in my life! Drinking is for morons!

MIMI'S VOICE: He hadn't touched the stuff until you called him ... after years and years had gone by ... to ask him for money ... crying

18

your eyes out! You brought him back on all fours at four o'clock in the morning! You don't have much of a memory, Sophie Guérin!

SOPHIE, *commanding*: Will you cut that out? … Mimi Panneton!

MIMI'S VOICE, *talking over Sophie*: You asked him to help you, and he did, then you laughed in his face … Because it's stupid to be a success … and have means … the means to help other people!

SOPHIE, *running out of patience*: Mimi! … MIMI! … *MIMI!*

MIMI'S VOICE, *talking over Sophie again*: You pissed him off this time, you really did! … And me too! … What are you waiting for? Applause? … For having taught us how to live? … All right: congratulations! You succeeded: we're depressed up to our eyeballs! Happy? Now will you leave us alone?

SOPHIE, *as Mimi sniffs back her tears*: Who do you mean, US? Me and who else? … Roger? Roger? … ROGER? … Holy shit! *(Mimi hangs up. Sophie hangs up, continues naming Roger, calling, searching)* Roger? … Roger? … Roger? … Is it over, Clover? Are you finished looting the drawers of those old bags down at the end of the hallway? Don't stop now, oodums poodums d'amour! Take your time, you no-count, worthless, blue-balled son of a goat! (…) (…) *(Smoking)* I won't miss his toothbrush in my rack! … This time he's going to kill me for sure! … *(The telephone rings)* Hello!

MIMI'S VOICE, *repentant, but still sniffling*: Hello. I'm … I'm sorry … I don't know what came over me, it must be the librium, the doctor told me it's supposed to calm me down … but it makes me twice as nervous. Real friends are rare and I don't want us to fight over some silly thing. Are you still mad at me?

SOPHIE, *stiff, disgusted*: I don't know. I'll tell you when I've thought it over. I don't have time now, I'm too nervous.

MIMI'S VOICE, *wounded again*: There you go! Look at what you just said. You're always laughing at people!

SOPHIE: Shit you're quick on the draw! Can't you listen to me a minute before you get all excited and untalkable to? (…) *(Mimi sighs)* I did a real dirty one to Roger … good and dirty … and now I'm scared shitless. I get up then I get down I figure I've got it made then I figure I'm finished I've gotta see you and touch you and talk to you ... Don't leave me all alone, come over, I'm afraid he'll cut me up into little pieces! (...) (...) DO YOU UNDERSTAND?

MIMI'S VOICE: *You* understand! Bernard is so far far down, he's torpedoing himself in the hold — on purpose. (...) He left with his contract, his insurance policy, his five thousand dollar deposit ... if he doesn't dry out before tomorrow night he'll lose the schoolbus maintenance contract. I know it's nothing for you, I KNOW ... but it's all we've got to get out of the hole with! *(She catches her breath)* If Bernard comes to see you, I don't want you to keep him, I want you to call me right away ... and don't give him anything to drink ... *(She starts crying again)* Is that too much to ask of you? DO YOU UNDERSTAND?

SOPHIE, *silent rage for a few seconds*: It's hard to UNDERSTAND. I'll need Roger to help me UNDERSTAND. And Roger isn't here ... *(Comical gestures of flying away)* Roger is gone. Upstairs. In his nightshirt!

MIMI'S VOICE: I must be the biggest drip on the block ... Not only do I not understand myself — it takes a whole team up to understand me! (...) Go ahead and say it, you think I'm a drip! I know I am but I can't get it into my head, I'm too much of a drip! Tell me, loud and clear!

SOPHIE: I won't, it'd give you too much satisfaction. I'd rather hold out on you! *(Mimi hangs up. Sophie hangs up. Already the doorbell is ringing; Sophie opens the door)* Next! ... Au suivant! ... Pull! ... Tirez! ... *(Having had the time to light another joint, she puts it out now)* Whoops! Scuze me! Rauchen verboten!

BERNARD, *comes skating in on one foot, a 40-ouncer of vodka in each hand, excited like a foolish virgin, opens his arms wide to receive an embrace; Sophie skitters away*: Don't you want to kiss me? ... Me who has crossed the desert to see you, walking day and night under a burning sun, without smoked glasses, not even a billed cap, just the shadow of a happy memory to shade my forehead: a wrinkled three-by-five snapshot from the days when you weren't so cool to me ... (...) I could have lost my sight, I could have COME BLIND, and you don't even give me a smooch!? ...

SOPHIE, *giving him a good kiss*: You're nuts!

BERNARD: I don't want a tight little kiss, I want a nice wet one, a real sweet one, a capital letter one with a three-dot fade-away ellipsis ... *(He entwines her)*

SOPHIE, *escaping his arms*: Go away, icck, you smell like a brewery!

BERNARD, *he catches her, he has all kinds of trouble with his 40-ouncers, he keeps spilling vodka everywhere*: That's not true, blue. I don't smell like a brewery ... I smell like a truery ... cause my heart is true to youery — and that don't stink! *(He takes her mouth; she resists a second then entwines him and shares the embrace)* Hmmm! If I'd known I would have come equipped with all my faculties! (...) But they wouldn't have wanted to come I know them they're a buncha spoilsports. *(He takes a swallow of vodka then offers his lips for the next kiss)* I'm ready for another, are you ready to give me one?

SOPHIE, *reticent*: Another? ... Or another then another then another then another-another I know you! It's none of my business but if I were you I'd watch my step: one drink makes you thirsty for the next and the second is never as good as the first.

BERNARD, *unctuous*: Cmon ... Cmon ... If you don't want to do it for me, do it for the starving Armenians ...

SOPHIE, *with Bernard's mouth on hers*: Okay ... but promise me that ...

BERNARD, *interrupting her*: Your mouth's too full of words! Swallow them and give me room to love you like I should.

SOPHIE, *in the end she does the kissing, one foot off the floor, the whole sorry business ... mocking him in the second degree ...*: Hmmmmm! Don't! Stop! HMMMMMMM Mmmmm! ...

BERNARD, *matching her ambivalence*: All right ... that's it ... I've found happiness. All right, that's great ... But it's too late ... I can't go on ... *(Turns tail and heads for the door)* there's no more road to travel on ... Well, so long now, the Mr. Nobody you gave everything to wishes you well, he's heading back, with regards from all the other

Mr. Nobodies who had everything then had to head back too ... because after paradise you take the blade.

SOPHIE, *catching him and directing him to the sofa*: No way ... (...) You're going to sit down and we're going to chat. I've been on the phone since Tuesday trying to find some real people, and all I get is Mimi with her histry and onyx. (...) A friend, specially a best friend, isn't just there to go kitchie-kitchie-koo: a friend talks! Now you're going to sit still and you're going to listen to me. *(She sits down next to him)*

BERNARD, *after an ironic belch*: What's the matter, Cupcakes? Whatcha got? ... A problem?

SOPHIE: You stoop! ... YOU STOOP!

BERNARD: A sek sek sekshual problem ... I hope.

SOPHIE: The only one I've got is the one you gave me and it's just like you: insignificant! *(They reach an impasse. She is mad; he is wounded. Then they both burst out laughing. He offers her one of his bottles. She takes it. They raise their bottles and clink a toast)* Here's to yours!

BERNARD: I prefer somebody else's.

SOPHIE: To somebody else's! *(They take a stiff drink, they laugh, then Bernard drops his spinning head in Sophie's lap)* We're laughing but it's not funny. I'm stuck, I don't know how to get rid of him!

BERNARD, *Sophie puts the bottle down at the foot of the sofa ... and makes a face*: Who him? *(Points to the Lazy-Boy)* HIM?

SOPHIE: If you only knew how long I've been putting up with it! (...) But it wasn't always all baboonery and platitudes. *(Bernard starts feeling up Sophie again)* He used to give me the craziest scares: I'd get up, I'd be trembling all over. He'd come out with the weirdest things, it made for a change of pace. (...) But now all he talks about is flops, things have got to flop, we've got to become the biggest flops in the world to set an example for others. The worst is ... he believes it! He says, "Call me Master, I'm the Master of Floppery," and he believes it ... *(Continuing as she pushes away Bernard's hand)* Can't you keep your hands off me for just five minutes? I'm talking! I'm talking!

BERNARD: I'm just trying to make you happy.

SOPHIE: Try with your ears for once! I'm talking!

BERNARD, *getting up*: Talk on! Talk on! I won't get in your way ... I'm going ... (*She grabs his head and puts it back in her lap*)

SOPHIE: Wait. You can hassle me in a minute. After I've given you a good excuse ... (*Lowering her head*) because I've got one ... it's all you need ... (...) Bernard ... aayyyyy ... Bernard I quit my job!

BERNARD, *getting up, pointing his index finger*: Ah ah! ... Ha ha! ...

SOPHIE, *with a show of practiced narration*: All weekend Roger was bugging me. Then I got to the office late again, and I got bugged some more. I couldn't stand it. The paté hit the fan. Shootout at the You're OK Corral! (...) I've been thinking about it for a long time. Hung up on money the way he is ... I said to myself: no more job, no more Roger ... two birds with one stone! I couldn't wait to see the look on his face: I took a taxi, it cost me eleven bucks. (...) He was there waiting with a brick wrapped in a towel. He read me the riot act for five minutes, his eyes were popping out of his skull, his forehead was creased like an old jacket — I didn't know what to do with myself, I was dying of laughter. He said (*Holding her nose, grinding her teeth together*): "I'm leafing. When I come back ... sooner than you think ... you'd better have put the joke back on. Or else I'll smash your brittle unemployment-assurance check and stick it up your nose! Have up in one nostril, have up the other!" *Sophie's routine sends Bernard into peals of laughter. She turns impatient, she shakes him*) What are we going to do? WHAT ARE WE GOING TO DO?

BERNARD, *laughter increasing*: Not much, not much ... we won't be able to ...

SOPHIE: If you're not a man, if you can't defend me yourself, call around, have contacts, get a hold of your guys, find me another job!

BERNARD, *getting to his feet*: Whoa now! Whoa Nelly get back ... Whoa! (...) I might not be too too steady on my feet but I know enough to get out of the way when the heavyweights come rolling by! If you want to run me over, sneak up slowly and don't be honking your horn like that! Whoa Nelly! ...

SOPHIE, *making demands*: *I* didn't say Whoa Nelly back there a minute ago! I made an effort! And you'll never know how much because I won't send you a bill! You turn up here whenever you want to, you slipper and slobber, you dangle around, you straighten up, you shrivel down, you make me put up with you, you think because you lent me your tricycle twenty-five years ago you can skip your turn forever! ... Well, it's your turn now!

BERNARD: Twenty-five years ago! *(He begins sobbing)* It can't be that long! Can it be, Cupcakes? *(She slaps him on the back, he takes another swallow of vodka that puts him back on track again)* You know ... since I've started drinking again, my name isn't too too good ... But Cournoyer, now that's a guy I've got by the short and curlies, no prolly ... *(He heads for the telephone)* He'll take you back tomorrow morning or he'll have to answer to me, no prolly, Solly.

SOPHIE: Forget Cournoyer ... I bashed him in!

BERNARD, *incredulous*: Father Cournoyer? What are you talking about?

SOPHIE, *having difficulty hauling Bernard back onto the sofa*: I gave him a knuckle sandwich ...

BERNARD: And you used to be so fiminine! ... Ah! You disillusion me!

SOPHIE: Don't you worry about my fimininity! If you knew how long Father Cournoyer's been catching me in a corner so's he can work his Roman fingers ... I'd have to have armor plate not to lose the faith ... Go to sleep!

BERNARD: If that's who you think my guys are ... I won't go to sleep!

SOPHIE, *putting a pillow under his head, coddling him*: All right, all right, they're not your guys ... Now go to sleep, go to sleep ...

BERNARD: If you say they're not my guys, all right ... I'll go to sleep.

SOPHIE: You going to be okay?

BERNARD, *as if he'd had a vision*: Yoouuuwwweee!

SOPHIE, *disgusted*: You going to throw up?

BERNARD: It's Mimi! She won't like me sleeping here. Yoouuu-wwweee!

SOPHIE, *reassured*: Who cares? She'll do like she always does: she'll histry, she'll onyx.

BERNARD: Yoouuuwwweee! ...

SOPHIE: You want me to call her? *(He nods yes)* She's going to ask about the car. Where's the car?

BERNARD: Down there ... in front of the house. On the stairs, on the steps ...

SOPHIE: I'm going to take a look. You have the keys?

BERNARD, *with a vague movement to his pockets*: Don't worry about that. Just worry about telling her I haven't had an accident. Not even a little dent. Not-even-a-little-dent, that's not much ... but Mimi's such a good kid that'll cheer her up. Not even a scritch. Tell her that. Because she'd better cheer up, you warn her ...

SOPHIE: What about your license? What about your wallet?

BERNARD: None of your beeswax ... Just tell her what matters: the bumper's still in front of the radiator. *(The lights go down. He's already snoring)*

SCENE 5

(The voices of Mimi and Bernard; Bernard, Sophie, Roger)

Bernard is in the bathroom, talking to Mimi on the phone. The lights will come up slowly and be full when their invisible dialogue ends. Meanwhile, we will see Sophie, who needs to go to the toilet, come out of her room, check the bathrooom door then sit down on the sofa to wait, chomping at the bit.

MIMI'S VOICE: Where are you?

BERNARD'S VOICE, *pitiful*: In the toilet. I didn't want to wake up Sophie.

MIMI'S VOICE: How do you feel?

BERNARD'S VOICE: Sick as a dog.

MIMI'S VOICE: Did you throw up?

BERNARD'S VOICE: I tried. Couldn't do it.

MIMI'S VOICE: Did you stick your fingers down your throat?

BERNARD'S VOICE: It didn't work. I must have made a hell of a racket. Hope I didn't wake up Sophie. She was awfully good to me.

MIMI'S VOICE: I see ...

BERNARD'S VOICE: I saved myself a finger of vodka to get me back ... It'll be okay ... If you're not too mad at me ...

MIMI'S VOICE: I'm not mad at you.

BERNARD'S VOICE: You're sure you're not mad at me?

MIMI'S VOICE: I'm just happy you called. *(She begins sobbing)* I was so worried!

BERNARD'S VOICE, *He is disgusted by her tears*: All right! … All right! … All right! … All right all right all right! …

MIMI'S VOICE: Are you coming home?

BERNARD'S VOICE: I'm not in the mood to have someone bawling in my ears. I feel bad enough as it is.

MIMI'S VOICE, *choking back her sobs*: I won't cry any more … come back …

BERNARD'S VOICE, *he's had some vodka, he'll have some more*: I'll come back when you start cheering up — and not before.

MIMI'S VOICE: Don't start drinking again right away …

BERNARD'S VOICE: The more you talk the further away I get. I better stop listening, I'm far enough as it is.

MIMI'S VOICE: I love you, I miss you, come to bed.

BERNARD'S VOICE: What for?

MIMI'S VOICE: To rest. I get tired too, you know …

BERNARD'S VOICE: I give you a lot of pain …

MIMI'S VOICE: It's more than just pain.

BERNARD'S VOICE: Pain with special sauce and a sesame seed bun?

MIMI'S VOICE: You give me what you have to give … It's not always the same thing …

BERNARD'S VOICE: (…) (…) What do you have on?

MIMI'S VOICE: The pyjamas you bought me. The white ones with the pinstripes, like the New York Yankees uniform. I put my watch in the drawer, I was looking at the time too much.

BERNARD'S VOICE: What are you doing with your hands?

MIMI'S VOICE: I'm holding the phone. I'm talking to you.

BERNARD'S VOICE: With both hands?

MIMI'S VOICE: Yes. I'm holding you with both hands.

BERNARD'S VOICE: You're sure you're sure you're not mad at me?

MIMI'S VOICE: I'm not mad at you, I'm mad about you. Even when you're there I miss you. Even when I'm lying next to you I don't get enough.

BERNARD'S VOICE, *his voice, that had become more and more tender, turns harsher and harsher*: You call that not-enough, do you? ... No bout adoubt it, you know how to place them. You don't need to tell me: I know my score's a great big goose-egg.

MIMI'S VOICE: Don't say that ...

BERNARD'S VOICE: Rubs you the wrong way, does it?

MIMI'S VOICE: (...) (...) Don't start up again, please!

BERNARD'S VOICE, *resolutely shooting himself in the foot*: What you don't understand is that I understand what it's like. When I was your age I hardly had time to button up my fly. Let yourself go, do what I did, take the car and get into cruise control! The streets are full of love, old love, new love, even black and blue love! With two bucks in the tank you've got enough for a sleepless night, getting tossed and turned on the bedpan of your choice.

MIMI'S VOICE: Bernard, I thought we'd settled that. You promised me we'd stop talking about it.

BERNARD'S VOICE: It's easy telling double amputees what to do when you've got two good legs! ... it's easy to stick out your tongue when you've got a pretty mug, say icky-poo that's not good enough for me, and sit on your sirloin till you're hungry enough to take a bite! ...

MIMI'S VOICE: I'm fat, is that what you're saying? (...) Do you want me to come get you in a taxi? ...

BERNARD'S VOICE: I want you to take advantage! Go out! Excite yourself! If men don't do it for you, try women, try groups, try it alone! Do something, anything! Holy virgin martyr, I can't do it! I'm not buying in!

MIMI'S VOICE: Be careful … I might just start believing you and really sacrifice myself. If I have to I can be the way you think I am, if I think you really want me to!

BERNARD'S VOICE: What's holding you back — besides warming up the car? I know — sewing. Let's talk about your sewing. You keep your prices so far down it costs me more than it makes you! (…) Display your pain! … I'm going to start believing myself too! *(Silence on the other end of the line)*

> *He hangs up sharply. Mimi hangs up. He tiptoes out of the bathroom holding the telephone that he will put back on its stand.*

SOPHIE, *very loud*: So?

BERNARD, *jumping out of his skin, then putting the vodka bottle out of its misery*: Holy shit you scared me! … Be careful, I just got beat up, I'm real fragile.

SOPHIE, *stiffly*: Flush it.

BERNARD, *dumbfounded*: What?

SOPHIE: I've been listening to you belching and slobbering and spitting and saying lamentations and woe-is-me's for the last hour. And you didn't even flush it … And I gotta go!

BERNARD, *hurrying to flush it*: All right! … All right! … All right! … *(Sophie rushes into the bathroom as he goes out)* Don't tell me I'm going to have the rare honor of hearing you do your tinkle-tinkle-little-star! …

SOPHIE, *through the bathroom door*: Don't count on it! I wasn't brought up in a barn! I wasn't towed into life by Panneton's Auto Body!

BERNARD, *the telephone is ringing; he lifts the empty bottle to his ear as if it were the receiver; he speaks into it as if talking to Mimi*: Panneton's Auto Body ... and Sons! Hello? (...) You're stuck? In the muck? Don't tell me, heart of my heart, that you're stuck in the muck again ... (...) Mimi! ... (...) Listen to me! How many times do I have to tell you not to drive into the ditch just because a big truck is on your tail? ... (...) Mimi! Let them do what they want! If they hit you it's their fault ... (...) *(The telephone stops ringing)* Go ahead! Be like that! Pull yourself out of the ditch yourself for once! *(He hangs up; he's had his fun. Sophie comes out of the bathroom with the sound of flushing water. He throws himself at her feet)* Give me a kiss!

SOPHIE, *matching his mocking*: A foot-kiss?

BERNARD, *leaping to his feet, caressing Sophie's mouth devotedly*: A real kiss!

SOPHIE: Okay. But let's get one thing straight ... There are some people going around asking for kisses, and when they get one, they start bellyaching about how it wasn't the right kind. What kind do you want?

BERNARD: Go ahead and beat me up, everyone else is!

SOPHIE: I'm not beating you up, poor thing. I'm just asking you what kind you want. I'm working at the counter, that's my job, I ask people what kind they want ... What kind *do* you want? *(The telephone rings. She rushes to answer)* Hello! *(On the other end of the line comes Vivaldi music and a cat meowing)* Hello! *(The other party hangs up. Sophie hangs up pensively)*

BERNARD, *gleeful, throwing himself at Sophie's feet again*: Wrong number! Another poor bugger who wanted Mata Hari and got Laura Secord instead!

SOPHIE, *in the process of deduction as Bernard lifts up her nightgown to kiss her ankles, her legs, her knees*: I know that routine ... That's the classical music and the Siamese cat meow from the old bag on the fourth floor. And that means Roger's winding up his tour ... And that means ... Bernard! *(Too involved in his licking to hear anything)* Is *that* the kind you like?

BERNARD: You bet!

SOPHIE, *mocking*: The PASSIONATE kind? ... Poor little teddy bear, you should have told me before! I've got warehouses full of that kind, they're on special this week, I don't have the slogans to sell them! *(Then she explodes. Throws herself on Bernard, knocks him over, covers him. Laces and embraces him, coos and moans, unbuttons and discovers him. The whole sad business of PASSION)* Want some more? Oh, yes, babycakes! Oh, yes, my little snake! Here! (...) There! (...) Mmmm! Mmmmmmmmm! Good, isn't it? Some more? Another spoonful? Have all you want! It's hot watch out! Heeeeere! ... (...) Mmmm! This spoon too teeny-weeny? Just a minute! ... Mama going to put on a bigger bib and use the soupspoon! (...) Here! Mmmm! Summore? I thought so! (...) Let's shovel it in. Summore? Say the word, little man! (...) Wait, Mama's running out ... Wait ... Mmmm ... Mama's going to give you the whole kettleful ... you can smear it all over your face! *(She gets up, with her feet on either side of Bernard's body. Just when, having peeled off her nightgown from bottom to top, she gets to her arms, she hears a sound at the door. She freezes, then covers herself up quickly)* Shhhh! ...Hurry it up!

BERNARD, *getting quickly to his feet, motioning to the Lazy-Boy*: You think it's HIM?

SOPHIE, *smoothing Bernard's clothing*: I don't think so, I know so!

BERNARD, *more annoyed than upset*: Okay ... where do you want me to go?

SOPHIE, *bravely taking up position in the middle of the room, facing the door*: Go in your pants! Like you always do!

BERNARD, *goes to open the door, stumbling, waving his empty bottle like a flag*: A guy that's just been run over by a truck ... he's dead, he's got no business being afraid ... *(He opens the door. Enraged, Roger comes in, the pockets of his bathrobe stuffed with balled-up newspaper clippings. He has eyes for Sophie only, he moves toward her, very slowly, taking a step, stopping to throw a couple of paper balls in her face, then continues)* Come in, come in! I drank the wine without choking, I ate the host without touching, you're just in time to ascend the pulpit! Mind the way up, the step is weak! *(He bows with a laugh to let Roger pass, then follows his step for step, aping him as he goes)*

31

ROGER, *to Sophie*: Didja didja didjado jado what I toldjato? …

SOPHIE, *she parries the first few paper balls with her hands, then drops her guard and attacks as much as possible*: Roger … Roger if you hit me again I'm going to call the police! Roger …

ROGER: Eyyyye I tole I told I toldja I warnedja!

SOPHIE: I'm warning *you*, Roger! I have a witness. If you lay a hand on me I'm going to the police!

BERNARD, *gleeful*: Don't worry yourself, Cupcakes, I'm here! I know plenty of lawyers, they'll take care of it! If he raises a hand, you won't have to lift a finger.

ROGER, *turning, pointing his fully outstretched arm at Bernard who retreats, hands clasped*: What's this stump up to? Is he up to aspiring beyond his station? Take this, you stump! *(He throws a paper ball at him)* And that! *(Another ball)*

SOPHIE: I forbid you to call Bernard a stump! He's my best friend! And that, pal, is called Hands Off!

ROGER, *his laugh turning into a bark*: Upsy-daisy, two mops scrubbing each other. Two Hoovers vacuuming on my rug! It's a scream! Turns me inside out! Makes me feel so unnecessary! *(His laughter ends abruptly)* Forget it. Where the woozy bruisy floozy fuzzy wuzzeye now? Heardja hurtja heardja quitjur job, goddamned bitch! Heardja hurtja walked right out the door! *(He yells)* What's wrong with you? *(He grabs Sophie by the shoulder, he shakes her)* What's wrong with you? What's wrong with you??? *(He throws her to the floor)*

BERNARD, *getting between the two of them, bottle raised threateningly*: Pick on someone your own size, if you're a man!

> *Roger disposes of Bernard with one hand, practically knocking him out. Sophie takes advantage of the uproar to run for her room. Roger catches up to her at the door and pushes her into the room. Noises, bodies falling, furniture knocked over, blows. He thrashes her and continues yelling.*

ROGER: What's wrong with you?

Sophie takes the punishment, she cries:

SOPHIE: Bernard!

BERNARD: Gotta go ... gotta go. That's my Cupcakes ... I'm obliged to go ... I gotta go. I can't not go, that's my Cupcakes: I gotta go!

Armed with his bottle, Bernard goes into the room. He brings down the bottle on Roger's head; Roger falls to the floor without another word.

SOPHIE, *her cry becoming*: Roger! Roger!

Sophie exits the bedroom quickly, followed by Bernard. She is wounded, torn, dazed; he is sobered up, dazed.

SOPHIE: You had no business killing him! I didn't tell you to kill him!

BERNARD: I didn't kill him, I just opened him up a little ...

SOPHIE, *going to wet a towel in the bathroom, with Bernard on her heels*: You split open his head this wide! That's not an opening, that's the end! *(The telephone rings)* Stop following me like a lap-dog and answer it. A drip like you, you probably killed him. Answer it, then call the police and tell them to come and take you away and hang you, I've seen enough of you, you drip!

BERNARD, *following Sophie as she returns to the bedroom with her towel*: You're bleeding, Sophie! Your face is all bloody! ... Do you want me to ...

SOPHIE, *interrupting him*: Don't worry about doing me ... Answer the phone!!! *(She stops, gives Bernard the towel, does an about-face while Bernard goes to take care of Roger)* Hello!

MIMI'S VOICE, *touchy*: You took a long time getting to the phone ... I hope I didn't disturb you in the middle ...

SOPHIE: Who do you want to talk to?

MIMI'S VOICE, *in agony*: Nobody!

SOPHIE: If you don't mind suffering another minute, I'll get Roger on the line. I can't put him on right now: your husband just butchered him with a vodka bottle and half his head is gone! But wait a minute … I'm sure if I tell him it's Mimi and that she's SUFFERING, he'll be right here! *(She puts down the receiver and runs to the bedroom door)* Roger! Roger! Mimi's on the line! SHE'S SUFFERING!

ROGER, *immediately emerges from the bedroom, his head wrapped in a bloody towel. He's having trouble staying on his feet but it doesn't show too much*: Hello …

MIMI'S VOICE: Roger? What's happened … again?

ROGER, *Guitryloquent*: What's happening right now … is you. And that hasn't happened yet, so this must be the first time.

MIMI'S VOICE: You're talking funny. What's the matter?

ROGER: Lucie's voice bounces like a ball in my ears when you say WHAZZAMATTA, and my bitch's whelp lights out after it. Tell me you didn't really say WHAZZAMATTA, show me the light, so I can call off the pup and call him to order! What are you doing with a stump anyway?

MIMI'S VOICE: What stump? What are you talking about? I don't have a stump …

ROGER: Oh yes you do. I see him everywhere. He's following me.

MIMI'S VOICE, *panicking*: What's going on? Are you really hurt?

ROGER: Perhaps you never knew … but once … one wintery month no doubt … I offered your arms the two sleeveholes of your coat so they could slide through with greater ease. And they went in eagerly, like two little trains into two little tunnels … as if your nails could not wait to be back in light again, so I could see them, like ten little eyes … That was the first time I touched you, the first time I hurt you.

MIMI'S VOICE, *panic increasing*: I don't get what you're talking about! I don't get it at all!!!

Roger collapses into Sophie's arms. She had felt him weakening from where she stood watching with Bernard, and had come running. Black out.

SCENE 6

The voices of Mimi and Sophie; Mimi, Sophie, Roger)

Lights up. Roger tests and retests this sentence on his tape recorder: "Transcend this surface from above: it is so slender, so smooth; were we to transcend this surface from below: I am so heavy, and you so low ..." Meanwhile Mimi and Sophie are happily gossiping as they climb the stairs. We hear their voices. When they reach the door, Roger flees to his room, disgusted.

MIMI'S VOICE, *curious yellow*: Really? ...

SOPHIE'S VOICE, *in fine fettle the whole time*: Then he asks me for 50 dollars ... He says he should have "most-favored-nation" status. He says that you just can't buy "old-style short-timers" like him any more now that "technocrats and gymnists have taken over the market."

MIMI'S VOICE: You're a scream!

SOPHIE'S VOICE: Ask him yourself! He's not shy, he'll tell you everything. (...) Anyway I'm not his only client: he's got every old bag on all four floors of this block ... He says *(She holds her nose to imitate Roger)*: "I'm not a girl of the streets, I'm a boy of the hallways!"

MIMI'S VOICE, *laughing, as if it were really a joke*: With half your paychecks and the odd job he does here and there ... he must have his pockets papered ...

SOPHIE'S VOICE: Let me tell you something: he's got a wad.

MIMI'S VOICE: A wad! ... You're a scream!

SOPHIE'S VOICE: Just as sure as you're born ... Money sticks to his fingers. He even goes through Bernard's pockets when he's drunk! I saw him doing it! I said, "What are you doing in there?" He goes, "I'm taking up a collection for Lucie's surprise party ..." Go ahead and look under his Lazy-Boy cushion ... if you've got a cast-iron stomach ... Cause it's good and thick in there ... Iichhhh!

MIMI'S VOICE: That's not what he told me about Lucie. He told me she was as ugly as a wart. He said, "I'm raising my bitch's whelp to bite the hole she's got in the middle of her mouth!" He's a scream!

SOPHIE'S VOICE: That's nothing! Wait till he starts talking about his two girls ... He'll show you their photos he's got scotchtaped to his heart ... Wait till he makes you sit them on your knees and dandle them ... He swears they're going to be prime mistresses. He writes them speeches ... then he records them. Sometime I'll play them for you. You'll wet your pants!

MIMI'S VOICE: I know what he does. And you shouldn't make fun ...

SOPHIE'S VOICE: Oh ... you already know ...

MIMI'S VOICE: (...) (...) (...) Hey Sophie ... Is it really true you make love ... paying?

SOPHIE'S VOICE: It all depends ... who with ... it depends on their vices ... How do you do it? Full of histry and onyx?

MIMI'S VOICE: Well, I'm ... Maybe I'm not quite normal. When someone touches me it hurts. If it's someone I don't mind, I pretend ... so I don't hurt him. (...) I'm so embarrassed ... I never mentioned it to anyone before.

SOPHIE'S VOICE: When they touch you where? ... When they touch you there? ...

MIMI'S VOICE, *very embarrassed*: Not there any more than anywhere else ... I mean ... everywhere. Even at the hair dresser's. Even when someone touches my hair. Once I went to the beauty shop. It hurt so much ... I never went back ... Even a handshake ... I try to keep it from showing ... I'm so ashamed.

SOPHIE'S VOICE: You shouldn't be.

MIMI'S VOICE: You don't think so? ...

SOPHIE'S VOICE: Whatever you do don't go see a doctor. You've got something special. I like it, it's phun!

MIMI'S VOICE: I know, *you* like everything ...

SOPHIE'S VOICE, *unlocking the door*: You bet!

> *Sophie and Mimi enter, each with a bag of groceries they put on the kitchen counter. A certain hesitation, a certain look shows Mimi's attraction to the Lazy-Boy's cushion.*

MIMI: Why don't you just be honest with Roger? Why don't you say, "Uhhhhhh ... I hate to hurt you but I can't stand you any more ...?"

SOPHIE : He'd grab me by the scruff of my neck and say *(Holding her nose to imitate Roger)*: "Wall, wall, walleye, howk howk howkum howkum you doan lub me any more? Wall, wall, bitch, of everything I taught you that's the only thing you remember?" *(She mimes Roger strangling her)* I'm the one I'd end up hurting!

MIMI, *laughing*: You're a scream!

SOPHIE, *starting to put away the groceries*: I bet you haven't laughed for a long time. Come on, help me, rattle your bones! ...

MIMI: What's that?

SOPHIE: I'm telling you to rat-tle-your-bones. That's one of Roger's expressions ... *(Mimi thinks that's a scream)* You go all excited soon as anyone says "Roger" ... What good is it to go all excited when no one can touch you?

MIMI, *quits handing Sophie the groceries; goes and sulks on the sofa*: You never quit! ... I rip my heart out of my chest, I tell you all my secrets, then you yank on the strings some more with a great big juicy smile on your face! Everything's one big joke to you!

SOPHIE, *sitting down next to Mimi*: I don't hear you quitting either ... You know we'll never stop being drips if we can't laugh about anything serious!

MIMI, *having thought about it good and hard, drawing her conclu-*

sion: We had a good time this afternoon. We did our shopping, we told each other our deepest fears, we kicked up our heels ... We were real close ... Then all of a sudden I get mad and start sulking ... You're right: I should change.

SOPHIE: You're too touchy, that's your problem. *(Mimi starts laughing again)* What are you laughing about now?

MIMI: Toochy ... I haven't heard it said like that since I left my father's house. We used to have a sawmill ... In Saint Mary Salome ... It was so long ago!

SOPHIE, *with the sound of claws scratching beneath her flattery*: Jumping Jesus you're sensitive! ... Most of us cry when we're moved ... But you giggle, like someone's tickling you under your arms ... You're so sensitive, you're ... you're ... I'm afraid to say innocent — you're so toochy it might bruise you.

MIMI: I don't understand, you're too cleaver for me ... You know what I mean?

SOPHIE: Are you drunk? ... Are you stoned? ... Are you regressing? You're so nervous today.

MIMI, *tragically*: I didn't want to tell you because I didn't want to ... But Bernard went to see the lawyer ... It's for real this time. We're going to lose the house.

SOPHIE, *stiffly*: This one or the one in the suburbs?

MIMI, *ignoring the attack*: We could have gotten out of the hole a little if we'd sold the car. But I don't want to. When you're in your house you're just stuck there: anything can come in and hurt you, you just have to take it. But when you have a good car nothing can catch up with you. Once you get rolling you go faster than the voices on the telephone, the news on the TV, faster than the machines that tally up the interest on your mortgage.

SOPHIE: Poor little teddy bears! Forced to sacrifice your garage — or your block.

MIMI: Our shares in the block give us just enough to put food on the table, no more. And the family went and put the garage in trust. I know you don't believe me, but in a week from now we won't even have a place to sleep.

SOPHIE: Twenty apartments and no place to sleep …

MIMI: They're all rented! The tenants pay their rent! You throw them out if you're so clever …

SOPHIE, *as though Mimi was complaining on a full stomach*: Since I don't pay I should throw myself out in the street first … but I'm too kind to do that to myself … We could find another way, what do you say? We have two bedrooms and two double beds … We wouldn't even have to get too close … And what if we had to double up? Among the poverty-stricken it's the thing to do … it's so heart-rendering! What are you waiting for, move in with us!

MIMI: You're so kind!

SOPHIE, *her tone of voice changing*: I don't know if you know, but I get along. I make plenty of dough on coke. We won't even have to tighten our belts.

MIMI, *getting up, grabbing her purse*: Cocaine! You sell cocaine!

SOPHIE: Good stuff, clean as a whistle … No bad chemicals, no downers, it's guaranteed. You want some? (…) (…) No? (…) I thought so … You come off better if your head's always square on your shoulders … just hold out until the downer goes away … and get depressed waiting for it to come back … (…) Don't leave …

MIMI: I think I parked on the wrong side … I'm afraid I'll get a ticket …

SOPHIE: You're safe on this side until six o'clock, I already told you. But don't listen, there's no percentage in trust … *(She takes her by the hand and leads her to the middle of the room)* Come on … I'm going to show you a little game. I know you'll like it, Roger made it up … Cmon … Cmon …

MIMI: Okay!

SOPHIE, *her hands behind her back*: Touch me. Five times.

MIMI: Where?

SOPHIE, *serious as a grave-digger*: Touch me. Five times.

MIMI: With my hands?

SOPHIE: With what you got. With what you are. With your feet. With a knitting needle ... With your knockers ... Oops, that's cheating, I'm not supposed to make any suggestions.

MIMI: I don't mind touching you. I just don't feel like it.

SOPHIE: I don't care whether you feel like it or not — participate. Play the game!

MIMI: What did you do when Roger made you play?

SOPHIE: You've got no ideas of your own, is that the problem? You just want to know the way other people play, so you can copy them ... Don't want to stick out too far, huh? Too bad, too sad, you're not playing with me any more. *(She crosses her hands in front of her)* Don't cry, I'm not disappointed ... (...) I always figured you were yellow.

MIMI: Give me another chance.

SOPHIE: What's the use? You've got to let yourself go, and you don't even have any go.

MIMI: I know, it's my fault.

SOPHIE: Don't hand mea those culpas.

MIMI, *trageometer rising*: My culpas are maximum ... I told you that on the stairs ...

SOPHIE, *holding her nose to imitate Roger ... and make Mimi laugh*: "Flyspeck, midden-heap, dung-beetle, shit de merde! Agane, agane, what is this pain? Is this the shitty end of the stick or what?" *(Mimi laughs despite herself. Sophie takes a bottle of ketchup from the groceries ... and begins to imitate Bernard, sending Mimi into greater peals of laughter)* Wait a while, wait a minute ... I'm going to do your husband for you. "Put on a pretty face hick! and lay down! I'm warning you hick! you better not hope for any home runs! Because hick! I've struck out again? Hick! I've been traded to the Exxxxxx-pos!" *(Mimi is laughing like crazy, that is, tragically)* You ain't seen nothing yet, babykins ... Wait till I imitate myself ...

MIMI: Stop! I'm dying of laughter ...

SOPHIE, *rushing to the door of Roger's bedroom, she lifts her skirt good and high, laughs and lets fly with her war cry*: Whisper!

MIMI, *as Sophie retreats with a speed equal to her attack, right into Mimi's arms*: He's coming out!

ROGER, *opening his door, looming on the threshold, a terrible vision*: Whassup, whassup, girlies? Lez keep it down, squirlies! Any way you Lezibeatens can keep it down? ... I'm asleep! Don't wake me up! *(He slams the door shut)*

SOPHIE, *taking Mimi's head in her lap. Mimi has fled, humiliated, deeply offended, and thrown herself on the sofa*: Don't pay any attention to him! ... You saw what he's like ... If you've got a weakness he'll sniff it out ... If you try to keep an eye on him, he'll hang out in the periphery and put it out for you.

MIMI, *throwing off Sophie's comforting arms as if they were twin tentacles*: Leave me alone! ... Leave me alone! ... I just told you, I can't stand that! (...) Roger's not doing it on purpose, you are! *(Over-expansive, she stops to swallow saliva)* Roger didn't spend the whole afternoon telling me all kinds of dirty stories to mix me up — you did! You're trying to use my weak heart — not Roger!

SOPHIE, *going back to the counter to put away her groceries*: Your heart's not what counts, honey! It's kidneys, pal, kidneys! *(She taps her temple with one finger)* Kidneys! Your heart never heaves enough to make it worthwhile! ...

MIMI: And what's this business about me having an eye on Roger? ...

SOPHIE: You don't have an eye on Roger ... do you? *(Puts her finger in her eye)* My eye! (…) *(Picks up an item from her groceries and gets set to pitch it* (Stand at the other end of the room: I'll pitch, you catch. *(Mimi is welded to the spot, she doesn't want to play)* Come on, do like Roger says: let's clone around, let's gust a butt!

MIMI: Go ahead, destroy our friendship, laugh it to pieces!

SOPHIE, *going off to play by herself. She begins throwing the rest of her groceries as hard as she can: cabbages, cauliflowers, carrots, porkchops, ham*: I'm letting you down, huh? (…) Don't be afraid! (…) Say it, I'm letting you down! (…) (…) Personally, I don't care. I'm okay. (…) Nobody can disappoint me, I don't have any points.

MIMI: Go on, don't stop. Laugh! Laugh at love, laugh at friendship. Laugh at sustenance.

SOPHIE, *coming to Mimi, hands clasped*: You're right, kit-kat. We're such good friends, such great lovers, such nutritious sustenances … and we destroy each other … it doesn't make sense.

MIMI, *pushing Sophie away*: Look at you! Look what you're doing … DON'T TOUCH ME! …

SOPHIE, *laughing, making little wasp motions*: I'm not zingy, I don't want to sting you … I'm hot, I want to warm you up!

MIMI, *in the doorway*: Your warmth gives me the chills.

SOPHIE, *getting down on all fours, like a dog*: I don't need to love you to bite you … Whaddaya say? *(She barks)* Huh? Rough! Rough!

MIMI, *holding the doorknob in her hand*: You're not in your normal state …

SOPHIE: Do you want me to say a poem to prove how much I love you? … Wait a while wait a minute … *(Mimi leaves. The lights go off)* "And the trees, surprised by nightfall, stand awake in the white darkness, dreaming …" Wait a while wait a minute … "Yet unacquainted with the world, wishing only for the cold breath of your frightful tombs, so low, so narrow …"

SCENE 7

(Sophie, Roger, Mimi, Bernard)

Lights. Sophie and Roger enter, dressed in Santa Claus suits. They wear long dirty white smocks down to their feet, on their backs they carry green garbagebags full of balled-up pages from the newspaper. In this scene, Sophie plays with Roger as if they were two children in an alley. She constantly changes tone of voice, language, attitude. She gesticulates grandly. She acts.

ROGER: Ha! Ha! ...

SOPHIE: Ha ha! Ha ha ha!

ROGER, *as they empty their bags in the middle of the room and sit down in front of the heap, facing each other*: Ah, our cook is goosed! Ah, we've had it! How about that? It fits perfectly! Let's act proud! ... Huh? Whadda whaddid whaja tellya? *(Holding his nose)* All we gotta do is hump right in. Rump right him.

SOPHIE: Holy mackerelshit! ... You bet! We're cooking with goose! Even if you had a hundred ladders no matter where you jumped you'd fall right in the middle! A hun'ed chairs! A hun'ed stools! A hun'ed picky fences! (...) *(Sweet-talking)* Roge ... Roge... it's really drippy playing flop with you. It's like phun!

ROGER: Dig in but stop dropdropdropdropdrop ... roproproproprop ... oodums poodums! ... *(Holds his nose)* ... drop a hold of Melpomene's rib already!

SOPHIE, *motormouthing, no stopping her*: Me: tragedienne! Me: aktruss! I need but rustle my lips to fashion the flow of cheap baubles that clatter in my mouth before they ever each my rears! ...

ROGER: Don't gobble, hobble, or I'll throttle! How dare you have "phun" ... HERE? There's no neon sign outside! You don't have to pull a muscle to get your money's worth — it's free!

SOPHIE, *chatting on as Roger unrolls some paper balls and reads them, very quickly, barely moving his lips, without using his voice*: Whaddaya mean? Isn't akting phun? What's the use of akting if it flops like in real life? (...) (...) *(Sweetly)* Oh, Roger, oh, Master ... and to think when I first came here, to this low place, I thought I was empty ... That I'd have to whip my noodle, and actually work ... invent a brand new me! To think of it! To think that the thirty-six set changes were already written in stone, that the whole drama had been scripted, revised, censored, staged down to the last detail .. and, oh Master, that we had been rehearsing it for centuries ... Master, you showed me I was full of my role, as round as a ball seeking a declined plane. Oh, Master, what caresses applied to perfect curves, what langor, what comfort! And the azzz ... *(She holds her nose)* azure horizzzzzz ... *(She holds her nose again)* zzzzzz ... *(Tries the nose business again, then breaks down)* zzzzz ... zzzzzzzz ... Help, Master, oh shit ... I've ... I've got ... I've drawn a blank! I can't remember where I put my memory!!!

ROGER, *imperiously pointing to the balled-up papers*: Everything you need to know is there! When there's no more left there'll still be some! It palputates, it pilulates, the rotators can't stop rooting. It's made to make sure that nobody ever has too big a blank to fill! No need to fear!

SOPHIE, *quickly smoothing out the balls*: Oh yes! Yes yes! I understand! Wait ... I want to play.

> *A dialogue of torn papers ensues. They take turns reading, at increasing speed ... Roger seated, recto tono ... Sophie standing, gesticulating, putting more and more expression into it until she reaches a kind of summit upon which she can sit, exhausted, and admire her feat.*

SOPHIE: "Riskowski tricked his hat! The Astros were too tough for the Roadrunners!"

ROGER: "Saint-Hubert, bungalow, five rooms, good location, electric heat, new paint!"

SOPHIE: "I'm thirteen years old! Two months ago I met a fourteen-year-old boy on Mount Royal! We spent the day together!"

ROGER: "Do you keep to yourself or are you sociable? Do you entertain often? Do your guests congregate in the kitchen or the livingroom?"

SOPHIE, *holding her nose to read these words*: "Our struggle against the Zionist enemy must continue as long as the entity called Israel occupies Palestinian land! declared Habash!"

ROGER: "At the opening ceremonies, several personalities posed in front of posters of Red Tomato and Little Bull, the mascots of the Métro Richelieu supermarket chain!"

SOPHIE, *with nose held*: "Our police officers are more and more unprotected! Captain Girouard stated!"

ROGER: "What are you thinking of, love?"

SOPHIE: "Better to say nothing! You of all people know that true happiness cannot be put into words! To accept it, to experience it totally — that's hard enough!"

ROGER: "The antiseptic decongestant vapors loosen your stuffy nose and ease your irritated throat!"

SOPHIE, *writing the figures in the air as she calls them off*: "The Conservatives captured 48.2 percent of the vote, against 45.6 for the Labour Party. This represents a 13.2 percent turnaround in votes!" *(She sits down in a heap in the pile of papers, throwing a few balled-up pages over her head, letting loose with her war-cry)* Whisper! Whisper! *(She's at her peak)* Ah, now that was something ... That was really it! Did you see how I interpreted it? ... Did you savor the fear that came squirting out? I didn't plan it that way: I just closed my eyes, I started to laugh, and it came out just like that: totally disgusting ... *(Roger pulls deeper into himself. He goes and sits down in his Lazy-Boy, begins rocking and nodding his head)* No aping, no going for effect! Pure, unadulterated heart and soul! Did you see it? Ta! Ta! Ta! Ta! Ta! Ta! Ta! Quick but not too quick! Like a machine gun that's slow enough to let you understand the bullets as they tear into your flesh! (...) I was having phun, I mean I was really having phun!

ROGER, *sinister*: Go ahead, knock yourself out, die laughing! Send in

46

the clones! Tiny talent night at the midgets' palace! A spoonful of Geritol and — bang — bring on Onan and his fabulous isms, the cart before the horse, plowing through the shit and licking the moldboard as she goes! Jawbreakers! All day suckers! Fol-de-rol I'm a troll! You can't touch anything without turning it into phun: the vilest substances, the greasiest gravics! Fol-de-rol, you're not droll! The Sportsman's Bar reel! Swing me from the bottom, I'm not too ticklish up top!

SOPHIE, *timorous at his first words; aggressive as he continues ... her rocking of Roger and his Lazy-Boy reaches dangerous proportions. As he swings his upper arms in troll-like motion*: I bet I've let you down again, huh? (...) I don't get what you got against phun! ... Joy, happiness, ecstasy ... I can understand you might turn up your nose. But phun ... the sheer horror of it ... its hideous visage ... you should get off on it ... Maybe you're missing something ... (...) I know, laugh and the world laughs at you ... so you're better off not enjoying yourself! ...

ROGER: No matter how you grasp an object, you always make it look smaller than it is! Stop trying to give things a tragic dimension: the labor is too much for you, you perspire and your sweat spoils your canvas ...

> *Suddenly, everything happens as once. The doorbell rings and Sophie rocks Roger so hard the Lazy-Boy flips over. The cushion and the money underneath shoot up into the air, as if on springs. Sophie and Roger end up on the floor as the money rains down. The doorbell rings with a vengeance. Sophie laughs, splashes among the riches, stuffs it every which way. While Roger panics and jams the bills into one of the garbagebags. The doorbell stops ringing. Bernard comes in, stewed as a newt, cigarette in mouth, waving a bottle of vodka ... followed by Mimi carrying two heavy suitcases, eyes floorward. When she raises her head and sees what she sees, she delivers herself of a scream.*

BERNARD: Ha ha! ... Ha ha! You mount a show and you don't tell a soul! You organize orgies then you keep them to yourself! Ha ha! ... Ha ha! ...

ROGER, *Stuffing, stuffing*: Shit! Shit de merde! Flyspeck! Dung-beetle!

BERNARD: You! Master! Down on all fours in the lettuce! Wait, I'll pitch in.

> *He throws himself into the "lettuce" and "helps" Roger by stuffing his pockets.*

SOPHIE, *laughing all the way, helping Bernard fill his pockets*: Hi, palsy-walsy! ... You want it we got it! *(Turning to Mimi)* Hi, walsy-palsy! What's come over you you see a ghost? You come here to crash? ... Shack up a while? ... Don't pay us no mind: crash, shack up! Make yourselves at home, palsy-walsies: crash, shack!

MIMI, *hysterical, still battling with her two suitcases*: Stop it! Stop it! Stop it!

ROGER, *still struggling with his money*: Oodums! Oodums poodums poodums oodums! Poodums oodums!

SOPHIE: Don't be afraid, Mimi! There's nothing to be afraid of! It's just a game! It's not real life! It's pretend! It doesn't really hurt! (...) Ask Roger ... Roger! Roger!

MIMI, *sobbing*: If you don't stop it right now I'm going to call the police! You're frightening me! What about simple human ecency?

SOPHIE: Poor thing! Roger! ROGER!!! You're forgetting "human ecency!" Show the guests to their room!

ROGER, *dropping everything, getting up, rolling out the red carpet and doing a few steps on it*: No, Bernie, don't move a muscle, guests don't clean house. *(Turning to Mimi)* Oh my God my God what a fallen gob! Sophie! SOPHIE!!! Too mush! Djou see the fallen gob Mimi's got?

SOPHIE, *coming running*: Too mush for sure! *(Patting Mimi's rump; Mimi drops her suitcases)* We'll have to get that gob up again! We're up to the job of that gob, you'll see, five minutes is all we need.

ROGER, *turning his attentions to Bernard, taking him by the shoulders, directing him toward the stereo*: That Sophie's a pottymouth, no bout adoubt it! Ah, she's a dirty one! Bet your legs are falling asleep, palsy-walsy. Wake them up before they start having nightmares! Here's how you do it! *(He puts on a little twist demonstration)* Come on, we'll roll out the barrel and cut a rug! What say?

> *While Roger puts the record player on, Bernard runs for cover in the women's arms. "Ti-Bidon" begins to play. As the lights fade, Roger begins dancing like man possessed, to general astonishment. Everyone is caught off guard.*

PART TWO

The set:
Same apartment, with changes in the furnishing to give it that "big surprise party in honor of Lucie" look. The sofa, stereo and Lazy-Boy have been moved stage right. They face the bathroom. A table occupies center stage and faces the audience. It has been set for Lucie and Lucie alone, as the single chair shows, but the service is for ten: food in different plates, wine in several glasses.

At the back, clearly visible: Polaroid-type photos of two girls (8-9-10 years old) blown up into posters.

The ashtray no longer flashes. Roger's semaphoric system is now composed of a siren and a policecar roof flasher mounted on the back of the Lazy-Boy. It runs only when he throws the switch.

The empty cupboard doors are open. The door to the empty refrigerator is also open.

The Characters:
The same. Living up to their Part One performance. Except Bernard who is less "well dressed," and who now wears glasses and has developed a tick: he rubs his mouth for no reason, as if he were wiping his lips.

Music:
Drum-rolls and the crash of cymbals.

SCENE I

(*Mimi, Roger, Sophie, Bernard*)

> *Curtain. Lights on Mimi and Roger who kiss ... with difficulty ... At the same time, though the two dialogues remain separate, we hear Sophie and Bernard talking as they climb the stairs ... as we watch Mimi and Roger.*

SOPHIE'S VOICE, *fed up*: When are you going to quit digging around in there? You excavating for a mine?

BERNARD'S VOICE: How can you turn down a massage?

SOPHIE'S VOICE: My ass aint no mailbox.

BERNARD'S VOICE: Not a mailbox, or not a female box? (...) Ha ha, got you there!

MIMI, *pushing Roger away gently*: I'm sorry, I can't do it. It means too much to me.

ROGER, *mad as hell*: I just got through explaining it to you! LET'S TAKE IT FROM THE TOP! All this stuff we're saying, and all this stuff we're doing — it's called love, understand? It's not the end of the world — it's the beginning! It's life's slowest scene, the safest and surest way to insure the dreary continuation of its stage business!

MIMI: There's no use explaining anything to me: I'll never understand!

ROGER: What's the problem? The idea is to go pet-pet like they did at the beginning of civilization and enjoy it like they do on TV! Now let's get going!

MIMI, *allowing herself to be entwined*: I don't understand why you insist on doing it with a drip like me. It'd be a lot better with Sophie.

ROGER, *as they begin to kiss with difficulty*: Everybody's got a cross to bear! And being a drip isn't Sophie's. I told you that already!

BERNARD'S VOICE: Once so fiminine ... and so vulgar now! I woulda never thunk it! A single illusion nourished me, and now it's been swept away.

SOPHIE'S VOICE: If it was your most nourishing, I'd hate to have to survive on the rest of them..

BERNARD'S VOICE: Whisper!

SOPHIE'S VOICE: Not wiss-puh-uh: hhwwiss-purr! Hhwwisspurr!

BERNARD'S VOICE: Hhwwisspuh-uh!

MIMI, *nuzzling back to Roger who, disgusted, had disentangled himself to go test his semaphoric system*: I know what you want. You want me not to feel anything when you do something to me. But it's not so easy not to react. We're not all the same. Some of our skins are ... very sensitive.

SOPHIE'S VOICE: Hhwwisspurr. Not puh, purr. Hhwwisspurr.

ROGER, *in a rage*: "Very sensitive?" That old saw? That old saw with crooked teeth that can't even saw its way through board-dumb any more? Oh Narcissus! Oh hothouse flower! Oh la la! *(The flashing light begins to turn. The siren begins screaming. As does Mimi, hands over her ears. Roger keeps the system working until quality control has rendered perfectly satisfactory results.)* It works. It's perfect. It's disgusting.

BERNARD'S VOICE: Hhwwisspurr! The hell with it! I never knew what to render unto hell when she came opening up before my very eyes, but now ... Now, now ... Whisper!

SOPHIE'S VOICE: Speaking of the devil ... how much did Roger give you for your shares in the block?

BERNARD'S VOICE: Block? What block? Oh, *this* block ... Mimi deals with him. I just signed, I didn't even read it. All I know is we're not drowning in red ink, and Mimi's stopped waking up in a cold sweat ten times a night to look outside to see if the process-servers have come to repossess her car.

SOPHIE'S VOICE: I bet she'd feel absolutely naked without her Thunderbird ... Poor thing. And don't you laugh either!

MIMI, *under the influence of the semaphoric system*: You know I'm nervous, you know that noise bothers me. I don't know what ...

ROGER, *hearing something at the door, interrupting Mimi who immediately puts a sort of giant baby-nipple on her head which falls down over her ears*: I hope you know your brittle speech by heart.

MIMI, *as Roger turns off all the lights except a spot on her ... and runs to the tape recorder to play the drumrolls and clash of cymbals that signal Sophie and Bernard's entrance*: Considering how long I've been rehearsing it ... I'd have to be a real drip ...

ROGER, *as Sophie and Bernard enter*: Ladies and gentlemen, Cows and Bulls, the new management of Clearview Apartments ... presents ... Mimi! In a brand new number! MIMI! ... Let's welcome her! Let's hear it! Don't just applaud her; inhale her!

> He makes passionate inhaling noises promptly and hilar-
> iously imitated by Sophie and Bernard.

MIMI, *surprising in her confidence and vivacity*: "My two-scooped brittle speech from the drone: one with saggy flesh fries, the other with foo flied lice. Two scoop soft stoop ice poop, two firm, round infirmities slowly melting down, lick'm'aids, the bitter sweet-tart of the heart. That with which we are here confronted, this is no simple game, no blame of inches, this is sport, with all the weight of the clerk's thumb hanging in the balance, with the arrogant will to antagonize the umpire and animalize the fans.

The game of blame when their side wins and takes off! clears the stands! Our stickhandles have no blades so's not to gain control of the pouncing buck.

The game of blame is to merge bicktorious! And depart! Let a chorus in one voice and unamimous carry them on their shoulders with the bitter taste of victory in their mouths! May they grant us respite! Leave us nice and komfy along the boards with the pouncing buck! They think I'm mincing my words. Mince! mince! they evince. Gargle it as throat rince! It's good for what hails you, good for your forked tongue and your mourning mouth!"

ROGER: End of the first scoop! Before digging into the second, let's stimulate our appetite centres by going Yum-yum. One-two-three! Everyone together!

> *He makes passionate yum-yum noises; Sophie and Bernard imitate him in peals of laughter.*

MIMI, *unfunny*: "The game is what sets us aflame. When they've beaten us as bad as they can and we fall ... down down down ... to the bottom of the heap ... far from the ashes of the heat of action ... unconscious. The game of blame is the ice that's left after they've triumphed, to a standing oblation ... and cleared out, left the place, each blinded by his blood ... No cups, no trophies; we'd be too wasted, too overweight, too shaky on our skates to hoist them! Our valor is measured against the grandeur of the empty rink, against the multitude of uninhabitable solitudes returned to the stands. The name of the game is to botch the match, for our cry of loss to fill the amphibeantheater. *(She gives a salute)* I bid you goodbye and wait for you to disappear!

> *She executes one last deep bow as Roger turns the lights back on and exclaims his enthusiasm.*

ROGER: That's wonderful Mimi! Too mush too mush too mush! That's wonderful that's great that's phun that's TOO MUSH! Can you believe your eyes, sprouts fans? Did you get your monkey's worth or not? Answer me? Huh!? ... Of course I thieved and extorted and out-and-out stole your money, of course I did! But you can't say I didn't do the right thing! You're such slaves to smoke and drink you would have thrown it away anyway! I saved it to save you, to transform your last rights into first places within a new culture. If you want to have guests you have to have a house, to have a big surprise party you have to have walls, and the dumb stones of these walls aren't about to tell those who come within them that they belong to us: that falls to the words on those walls, and the words that Mimi read are among them. *(Sophie and Bernard laugh like madmen)* And those words flew from my own pen! If I may say so myself!

SOPHIE, *pulling Bernard into the bathroom*: Come on! It's inter-emission.

ROGER, *with held nose, addressing himself to the door ... that has just been slammed in his face by Sophie and Bernard*: And you are my interemitters. You have heard my word that salvation is a salad best eaten cold. Colder. Coldest.

MIMI, *takes off her nipple, throws herself on the sofa, discouraged*: Looks like we flopped. Our number didn't fly. It crashed. Like a ton of bricks.

ROGER, *enthusiastic, on the contrary*: A ton of bricks makes an oven. It was hot, I'm telling you, really hot! But since we were hoping for a double blank, you can't say we didn't hit the nail on the head. Anyway, a little chin-uppance! What did I tell you our goal was when we put on this low farce?

MIMI: A climax.

ROGER: An *anti*-climax. And a flop is always the high point of an anti-climax. So?

MIMI, *getting up, pacing after him*: Everything's gone and turned uncomfortable again. Uncomfortable! Always uncomfortable! We've been together for three months and we haven't had a day without discomfort. I'm sick of it!

ROGER, *angry*: If you're looking for happiness find yourself another guru! Go swim in your stump's backwater, your stump's or some other stump's! Every stump knows that happiness means getting as much phun as you can and if you don't there's no sadder fate!

MIMI, *pointing to the door fearfully*: Shhhhhh! Don't talk so loud. It breaks my heart. He's had a hard enough time as it is. He's been shamed enough.

ROGER, *louder, with violent gestures toward the door*: Shame? That stump? Who has nothing better to do than giftwrap himself in that slut's skirts at the first prick of the heat?

MIMI, *with one hand on Roger's mouth, trying to appease him*: Shhhhh! Not so loud ... you nasty thing. You make me see stars ... and I've seen enough as it is.

ROGER, *pointing to the door again*: A slut and a stump! And the opposite is inversely true! She sluttifies him! And he stumps her. Oodums! Oodums poodums poodums! Poodums oodums! Everybody's doing it! They do each other, they undo each other, they deform each other then they reform each other! The zombie jamboree!

MIMI, *awkwardly throwing herself around his neck and kissing him greedily*: Shhhhh ... (...) Your mouth tastes like fire ... you're a devil ... (...) I like it that way. It's good that way.

ROGER, *he entwines her too hard, Guitryloquent*: Hold on tight, love. We'd better hold on. If we don't let go and everything works out ... which means bass ackwards of course ... one oven igniting the other into a deculminating process ... for in the oven of our love our deculmination will culminate for good ... in other words the deepest darkest bottom of the black hole of phun ...

MIMI, *after another difficult kiss*: You said love. I'm sorry, I don't want to hurt you, but I never said I had any love for you.

ROGER, *not hurt*: Really? ... What *do* you have?

MIMI: Cum passion.

ROGER: Cum quat? Cum cum what?

MIMI: I have for you what I have for myself: regret for what I didn't do well, and desire to never do anything again that I could ever regret. Cum passion.

ROGER: I wasn't asking you for that much, but why not, it adds up to the same thing: STOKE THE OVEN!

MIMI: I know what you think. You think everything's been fixed ahead of time. Nothing can possibly come along that hasn't been aiming its malevolent little self at us for eternities. You think nobody really decides anything, especially not me. Remember that time I fell into your arms? I know you weren't surprised. On the contrary! The usual tedium! But I don't care: you're wrong! I didn't fall into your arms because I thought you were handsome and intelligent and the usual tedium. I did it because we were both so pitiful apart, and worse when we got together ... and it was horrible to hurt that pitifulness. Especially you and your Brittle Speech with two scoops. I put my hands over my ears when you taught me it and I saw it for what it was. The only eruption was your breath, your puny respiration, scarcely stronger than mine. Only I could be upset by such petty strength, and I can't stay on my feet anyway. So pitiful compared to the volcanos you thought your insults would conjure up. You thought they'd spring up like mushrooms and heave like tidal waves — it choked me up and I couldn't say no. It's not my fault, when a man inspires pity in me, I'm his. His! When it comes over me I can't keep from giving him everything I happen to have at the time.

ROGER, *moving aside, as if frightened*: Do you feel it now?

MIMI, *in total honesty*: I do. And I'm afraid just how far I might go.

ROGER, *coming closer, feeling the temptation*: Don't tell me I have you ... Oodums poodums!

MIMI: You do. But I won't kiss you any more. I've given myself enough as it is. You have me but that's as far as it goes, I can't go any further. It hurts too much.

SCENE 2

(*Sophie, Roger, Mimi, Bernard*)

Black out: Bernard rattling in his sleep, sick as a dog. The night is almost over. Everyone is bedded down: Sophie in her room, Mimi and Bernard in Roger's ex-room, Roger on the sofa.

SOPHIE'S VOICE, *hollering, hitting the wall*: Mimi! ... Mimi! ... Flip-Flop!

MIMI'S VOICE, *half asleep*: Yes, Sophie! Yes!

SOPHIE'S VOICE: You need help, Mimi?

MIMI'S VOICE: No, everything's okay. Thanks anyway, Sophie!

SOPHIE'S VOICE: You sure you don't need a little hand ... For sure-for sure?

MIMI'S VOICE: For sure-for sure!

SOPHIE'S VOICE: How bout a foot?

MIMI'S VOICE, *yawning*: A foot?

SOPHIE'S VOICE: Yeah, to kick that thing out of bed! Don't you think he's come enough already? My alarm's set to go at seven and I haven't been to sleep yet! Jesus Christ! (*Mimi is quiet under Bernard's heaving and rattling*) Holy shit! (*Sophie provides a loud imitation of Bernard's noises*) That son of a blue-balled blessed fly-flicking flick-flacker!

> *Sophie opts for getting up. Lights. She comes into the livingroom in her nightgown, rattling along with Bernard. She makes coffee, slowly starts getting ready to go to work.*

SOPHIE, *shaking Roger as she goes by*: Hey Junior! Junior! Whatcha doing there, old sock old noodle old bean? *(He grumbles)* I don't want to disappoint you, but I've got bad news for you: you smile in your sleep!

ROGER, *turning over, pulling the covers around him*: Flyspeck! Middenheap!

SOPHIE, *going into the bathroom, singing the Saint Hubert Bar-B-Cue jingle, talking to Roger as she brushes her teeth*: "Where do I go cause I know about chicken?/Where do I go now I know that there's more?/That's cause I know that there's more to enjo-o-o-y!..." Hey Junior Mints! You'll never guess who I was out whoring with last night down at the Sportsman's Bar ... (...) Your very own Lucie ... Sure's you're born! Your Lucie alias My Eye personally and in person! That sets you back a step, huh, Junior? Now I know why you didn't want me to go back to the Sportsman's. She's the toast of the tushies down there. The guys call her Luciefer. She thought she'd put you out in the street for good. She was real broke up when she heard we'd picked you up and that we were the ones about to end up in the street. Anyway, don't worry about having to find her so's you can issue your invitation: it's been done. She said YesnomaybesoI-dontknow. Let me give you a piece of advice: don't push it. Because I get the feeling that if there's going to be any surprise parties thrown around here, she's going to be doing the throwing. Besides, with the appetite on her, she's not going to go for that crap sitting out there on the table going stale.

ROGER, *waving his arms in the air, totally disgusted*: Great! Just great! The cart axle to axle with the calving cow! Fertility encopulated, rich gestations! Well? Well? You happy now? So let me sleep! *(Turns over again and wraps himself up in the covers)*

SOPHIE, *shaken but pushing on, continuing to turn the knife. She shuttles between the sofa to the bathroom and the kitchen, fixing her hair, putting on her make-up and making coffee simultaneously*: What a fizzle stick! Never seen anything like it! She's a spit on the image *(Pointing to the posters)* of herself as a little girl! When I told her how you had us believing you'd had the girls together, she almost fainted. When she got her senses back we both figured it could have just as well been moving, instead of disgusting ... (...) Fizzle stick! And vulgar! Vulgarian! Vulgate! Vulgus! Vulturine! Then she grabbed both my hands and she said: "I don't know how you can stand him. Not that I want him back again, but if you can't get rid of him any other way, I'll sacrifice myself. He'll pick up and fly, it'll be my favor to you ..."

> *Sophie goes into her room and slips on a dress. She rattles along with Bernard a while. Then slaps the partition and yells.*

SOPHIE: Mimi! ... Mimi! ... Flip-flop! *(No answer)* "He got me down on the floor and he wouldn't take no!" You know what time he started? *(...)* You know what time it is now? *(...)* Give him his bottle, do something, shit, Mimi! Babycakes! Flipflop! *(No answer. Sophie desecrates a Joni Mitchell tune)* "He was shakin' and bakin' and he wouldn't take no!" *(Sophie comes out of her room, rattling along with Bernard, then zeros in on the sofa, it's Roger's turn)* Hey, Junior Mints! Junior Mints! Junior! I was digging your cushion the other day ... Out of compassion, rest assured, I thought you were busted ... But Christ on a Bike! ... I had to hold my nose with both hands! ... But-but-but! ... How did you get that much so quick, all slacked out in your chair like that?

ROGER: I lower myself when the whores go by: they drop everything.

SOPHIE, *reaching the bathroom*: I know plenty of real pimps. They're not much to look out, but at least they don't foul their nests!

ROGER, *making it to Sophie's door*: All Petri dishes being equal, I'd just as soon bite myself with my rotten teeth and suck the sores than come all soft and scrawny in your muddy delta. I'm a poet! A poet! Understand? *(He slams the door)* Po-it! *(He locks the door)*

> *Bernard rattles. Mimi's sleepy murmuring comforts him. Sophie emerges from the bathroom and carries five or six empty vodka bottles to the garbage can in the kitchen.*

SOPHIE: Poet, poet, poet, poet.

> *The coffee is ready. Sophie pours herself a cup and takes a sip. Then she takes up position in front of Roger's locked door.*

SOPHIE, *derisively*: Poet, poet, poet, poet.

ROGER, *from his room*: Not poet, po-it.

SOPHIE: Po-it. *(Sophie turns round and round, rattling in unison with Bernard. Then she changes target again.)* Mimi? ... Mimi? ... Flip-flop??? (...) *(No answer)* "I'm down on the flo' and I won't take no!" *(Meanwhile Bernard comes out of his room, suffering, whimpering, stumbling, followed by Mimi who holds out his glasses, charitably, awkwardly.)* Where do you think you're going?

BERNARD: Whoa Nelly! Don't raise your voice. It's bad enough having the floor on my case! *(He points to the floor, then drops to it on all fours)* You didn't believe me, huh? ... you see that? ... you saw it ... good thing I caught myself, it wanted to jump in my face! *(He curls up on the floor, he grabs his head, palms on his temples)* I suffer! I suffer! Ah! Ah! Aahhh! I suffer! ... Aahhhhh ... I can't take it any more. *(Ah, he's really suffering)*

SOPHIE: If it's too much, stop putting up with the indignity: die, DIE!

BERNARD: Gee-zus, with everything else going on, I forgot all about that option. Not a bad idea. I'll do it. *(Writhes with pain, weeps)* I'M GOING TO DIE! ...

SOPHIE, *vainly trying to get him back on his feet, ceding the glasses again to Mimi*: Another problem fixed! Goddamn we're moving right along this morning! We're really cooking with gas! *(Then she turns angry, yells at Mimi)* Is there any way you can get those two hands of yours to work? Stop standing around gritting your teeth and looking tragic! Lend me one of your wringing hands, he's going to soil the rug again! ... I know, you don't care — the po-it isn't going to terrorize *you*!

BERNARD, *attempting to stand up on his own; unable to; struck down by the voices; head shattered by sounds*: Not so loud. Not so loud. *(Supplicating)* Don't yell ... I know I've given you plenty of grief, but don't yell, it's almost over, I'm finally going to die. I'm just about there! (...) Mimi? Mimi? Are you there, Mimi?

MIMI, *kneeling down, finally able to put Bernard's glasses on his nose*:

I'm here. I won't abandon you. Wait. I'll get you a nice cool washcloth.

BERNARD, *hanging onto Mimi*: Don't go away, Mimi, don't leave me. I know you don't love me any more but I don't care, at least you don't abandon me, you don't yell like they do ... You know I really am sick.

SOPHIE, *getting up and going into the bathroom*: Don't worry ... I'll go. Phew! I don't know how you can sleep in the same bed as that thing. Yeech! ... He opens his mouth and you've got to air out the whole house! Jumping Gee-zus whatchew got in there? Poor Flip-Flop!

BERNARD, *Mimi sits on the floor, raises his head, puts it on her thigh, strokes it*: Don't yell, oh please love don't yell.

MIMI: I'm not yelling, love, I'm not yelling. Don't cry, oh please love don't cry, don't cry.

BERNARD, *attacked by nausea*: That's it, I can feel it, I'm dying now, I'm dying.

MIMI: Hold it back just a little bit more. Wait. Don't throw up on the rug. Sophie is bringing the yellow bowl.

ROGER, *emerging from his lair, unpeeling Mimi from Bernard, pushing aside Sophie with her washcloth and vodka and yellow bowl*: When are you going to cut the flack so I can relax? Huh? Be off, harpies! Unfasten your claws, stay your beaks; what's this mack attack, Jack? (Picking up Bernard who utters death rattles, carrying him into the bathroom with no further ado) You don't play in slop, you shovel it up, you don't dirty your appendages in it, you make fast work of it, like this! (Sounds of Roger tossing Bernard into the bathtub and turning on the shower. Coming back and heading for bed again) Now are you going to cut me some slack? Now are you going to let me relax?

> *Mimi picks up the bottle of vodka and drops into the guest chair. Since there are no other chairs in the vicinity, Sophie, after getting her cup and tickling Mimi on her way back, sits down on a corner of the table.*

SOPHIE, *in fine fettle*: Are you sulking, sulky? Are you sniffling, snoopy? Christ, what a morning!

MIMI, *awash in pain*: I'm not sulking and I'm not sniffling, I'll have you know! (*She takes a swallow of vodka*)

SOPHIE: That's right, take a little taste, makes your monkey jump.

MIMI: I'll take as big a taste as I want! As much as I want when I want! (*She takes a really big one then bursts out sobbing, weeping like a Sorrowful Mystery, clutching bottle to breast*)

SOPHIE, *nasty*: How come you gotta cry, honeybuns? Huuuh? How come? Don't you feel good? Your tushie's all wet and it gives you an owie? How come you gotta cry? Cause Mamma got up and hadda change your die-per?

MIMI, *wiping away her tears like greasestains, taking another taste — she'll drink through the rest of the scene to irritate Sophie*: Why are you yelling at the top of your lungs like a witch in heat? Who're you trying to wake up?

SOPHIE: The devil, that's who! Don't you think we could use a little devil here? Don't you think we're unworthy of knowing true unhappiness? That if we were really so unhappy we wouldn't be such cowards?

MIMI: Don't waste your breath asking me. You don't play in slop, you shovel it up. (*Sick laughter*)

SOPHIE: Now you're laughing! Ha! Ha! Ha! You're so yellow you make me sick! (…) I'm warning you: if you don't get mad sooner or later, if it never comes out, we're going to have to throw in the trowel and figure you just don't have it in you: you're as priggy and prissy on the inside as you are on the out, a stoop from recto to verso! (…) Do you have any guts, Mimi?

MIMI, *in a fit of laughter that launches the mouthful of vodka she just took in*: No! (*Rubbing her stomach*) There's absolutely nothing inside! Nothing to wound, nothing to bleed, nothing for you at all. (*With a frown*) Zilch! Nichts!

SOPHIE: I pity you ... And you like it so much I'm going to tell you again: I pity you. And you're not the only one in this mess I pity ... *(Points toward the bathroom where the shower is still running)* What about him? Aren't you going to look after him? I suppose it'd be more pitiful if he drowned.

MIMI, *protesting too much*: I don't give a damn! He can drink, he can dry, he can live, he can die, I don't give a damn! I don't give a damn about anything! Nothing makes any difference to me! *(Crying)* I'm sick of acting hurt, I'm sick of pretending to cry! *(There, now she cries a little)*

SOPHIE, *getting worried, going to see how Bernard's doing*: Should I go and see?

MIMI, *another taste has changed her mood*: I couldn't care less! And the more I care less, the better it feels! (...) Now that's something! Now that makes sense! *(Meanwhile, in the bathroom, Sophie turns off the shower as Bernard laughs, teases and splashes her. Mimi rises to drink a toast to indifference; she's not too steady on her feet)* Whoops! A toast to I-don't-give-a-damn! Now that's progress!

SOPHIE, *coming back with a wet dress*: He's got his bottle, he's okay. (...) Good thing I went in there, the bath was getting pretty full. He asked me how come only the water on the top floats, and how come when he pushes it down it springs back up again, even though the water underneath falls back as soon as he lifts it up. He's having his fill of fun. *(No answer)* How about you?

MIMI: How am I doing I'm all right. How about you? You like your new job?

SOPHIE: I sure do. I fell in with a real good gang. All of them young, just about. Peppy ... hungry ... With the kind of eyes that shine and spy and beckon: "Come here let's get together ... let's get in some trouble ... where it's hot, where things are happening!" Get the picture?

MIMI, *starting to giggle again*: We must be pretty boring.

SOPHIE: Too boring for words. And if you start drinking too, that'll be the end, finito: next time we go to take a bath, our feet'll float on the top instead of our heads.

MIMI, *laughs again, then collapses, drunk and exhausted*: It's all right by you, you get up in the middle of the night to look for trouble, but I'm falling asleep. I want to go to bed. *(She gets up, wavers, leans against Sophie)* And not alone either, no bed all alone, I couldn't stand it ... With my husband! That's right! (...) But I need a taxi; can you drive me? *(Sophie takes her by the waist and leads her into the bathroom)* Hey, cmon now, Sophie, don't turn left when I want to go straight ... I know you, you're sleazy, don't lay me down in just any guy's bed ... Don't steal my fidelity, it's my only virtue.

SOPHIE: Cmon, Flip-Flop, get it in gear.

MIMI, *halting the convoy to finish developing her thought*: I'm stuck here, I never go away, I'm like a stubborn stain ... It's all I've got. Promise me you won't take it from me, promise me you won't hold out on me like Sister Teresa used to! "Are you there, Mimi!" "Yes, I'm here, Sister Teresa." I loved her and she always held out on me: "No, Mimi, you're not there, you're in the clouds!"

SOPHIE: Follow me, sweetie ...

> They go into the bathroom, greeted by Bernard's trium-
> phant *"Whisper"* and a great splash of water.

MIMI'S VOICE, *falling into the bathtub*: Look out below!

SOPHIE'S VOICE: Not my hair! Don't get it wet, I just fixed it! My hair!

MIMI'S VOICE, *baby-talk*: What's your name?

BERNARD'S VOICE: Broomstick! What about you? What's you name?

MIMI'S VOICE: Mine's Flip-Flop!

SOPHIE, *coming out of the bathroom amid peals of laughter, generally disgusted*: Gee-zus Christ!

SCENE 3

(*Sophie's voice, Mimi, Bernard, Roger*)

Black out. Sophie and Mimi are going out for a night on the town, they're in the mood. As they go Bernard calls after them, "Don't drink too much now!" Sophie answers, "We're not going for booze ..." Then Mimi joins in: "We're going for meat!" Lights. Roger is sitting in his chair, writing. Bernard is pacing nervously, wiping his mouth, embarrassed at the frequency with which he returns to the bathroom, on whose door hangs this sign: SAVE YOUR SOLES — DRINK HERE. We hear Sophie and Mimi's dialogue as they go down the stairs.

MIMI'S VOICE: I'm not too crazy about the idea, I don't mind telling you. I'm not much fun. I find a chair, I sit there, I can't think of anything to say.

SOPHIE'S VOICE: Don't worry about it. The guys do all the work. They're just dying to.

MIMI'S VOICE: I'm a useless appendage. I never know what to do with my body.

SOPHIE'S VOICE: Don't say that. You've got a car. You know how to drive. You'll take us to Lovers' disco in Sainte-Rose. It's phun there. It's real kitsch.

BERNARD: The girls go out and the guys stay home! That's the Women's Movement for you! The union of wounds and swellings! Well, I might as well stop talking if you aren't going to answer. (*He goes into the bathroom to take a nip*) Hey, Master! ... (*He comes out of the bathroom as Roger starts testing his text on his tape recorder*) Master? ... Master? ... Master, are you for the women's movement? (...) I'm for them moving ... right out the door. But I won't send them out in the street without a shirt on their backs ... Let them have it all: our insurance companies that take away our houses, our general motor that pollutes our lungs, our hospitals on the critical list, our agriculture that grows nothing but quotas — let them move out with all our junk! (…) Let them clean house and clean it good for once! *(He laughs)*

ROGER, *reading loudly as if Bernard was not there*: "We tried all our keys; they broke off in your locks, they whittled away to nothing. We're finished, we'll never escape … Your walls pursue us when we flee and precede us when we stop; your gates recognize us, whatever mask we adopt …" *(Tears up his text angrily)* That's me! What kind of mack attack ack ack trash is this? Me put that kind of trash in the mouths of my children! Shame, shame, for shame! Mush, mush, for mush. I've sunk low enough as it is: I won't stoop to putting the burden on those who have no shoulders to bear it. *(He begins writing again with renewed ardor)*

BERNARD: Before I was a stump! Now they've taken away my shoulders!

ROGER, *getting unhinged, engaging in conversation*: Listen, I've screened your test: you flunk. Don't bother primping and preening: I won't produce you! You can put your briefs back on: you're not photogenic enough, I won't let you on my stage! *(As Bernard goes into the bathroom again to wash his face, Roger writes:)* "Brittle Speech from the drone locked in the toilet *(He scratches out "toilet")* in the bathroom *(He scratches out "bathroom")* in the washroom *(He's tired of scratching out, he's mad)* in the shithouse!" Flyspeck! Middenheap! What language do I speak anyway? Fuckenhell can't even talk right to my own kids! Too too. Mush mush. *(He begins writing again; Bernard comes out of the bathroom)* I've got to push I'm getting close I can feel it!

BERNARD, *the more he drinks the more confident he becomes*: What are you writing there, crab-louse? Your next part? The part of the crab-louse?

ROGER: That's right, I'm writing my life ahead of time, I'm choosing it before someone else chooses it for me, or before it chooses itself, like the Zens say. I want to pull my own strings. I'm a creator — my creator; I predict myself!

BERNARD: All right already! Let me tell you something, Don Cherry, and that something is all I'm going to say, and here it is: everybody …

ROGER: Everybody is what he hears. To make the world, you just have to stand up and take the floor, you have to be what the world thinks is happening to it. If you hang back in the crowd it's over you'll always be a listener. And get done to not do. You don't act in a crowd you react. You don't actate you reactate, you don't play you watch.

BERNARD, *pacing and wiping his mouth with increasing nervousness*: Don't bother! All you're proving is how you think everyone else is a cartful of empty suitcases! The reasoning of a cretin! I flunk you! *(Stops in front of the bathroom)* I'm going to absent myself! I'm giving you thirty seconds to rework that draft! *(Goes into the bathroom, comes out immediately)* If you can't reason any better than that I'm knocking you down a class! *(Closes the door then opens it again)* I'm lowering you in my estime!

ROGER, *gets up and walks*: That's it! I've found it. Completely by accident! *(Rising in ardor, actating)* "My children, my dual daughters, I want you both to be prime mistresses, to speak the writing on the walls and be what cracks their mortar ... Anything ... As long as you're not standing underneath when they come tumbling down." *(He sits down and starts writing again, excited)*

BERNARD, *slipping quietly out of the bathroom, mischievous*: Whisper! *(Roger is startled in spite of himself)* Howdy-doody-do? Howdy-doody doin there? Ha ha! ... Ha ha! ... I rattled your cage one there now, didn't I do? (...) Pisses you off yellow, doesn't it do too, me making jokes while you're having a crisis of creation? Dis dis dis disgusts you don't it? ... huh, you dictator, you emperor, you Hitler, you delusion of grandeur? (...) I'm warning you: if you want me to throw myself on the floor and cry! You'd better put me in jail and take away my red-eye! *(He eggs on Roger as if teasing a dog)* Cmon! Cmon and try! Doggy-doggy-puss-puss! *(He gets down on all fours and he'll stay that way until the end of the scene, more like a monkey than a dog, even if he does bark)* Woof! Woof! Try and catch me! Just try! Woof! Woof!

ROGER, *relighting his cigar*: You're all mixmastered up! You're sniffing up *my* tree, not vicey-versy ... You're the one coming on batting your big eyelashes ... You don't need me anyway: you screw yourself up well enough yourself thank you very much.

BERNARD, *returning to the bathroom*: Kids say the darnedest things ... But don't think I'm about to throw in the trowel ... I'm just going to consult the spirits...

> *Black-out. As if we are with Bernard in the bathroom, with his death rattles, his pain and misery, his sighs, his gurgling, his belching.*
> *Lights. Bernard coming from the bathroom, not nearly as acrobatic on his four legs. A lot of time has elapsed.*

BERNARD: The spirits agree with me. The world is divided into two types: suitcases and sponges. Both are made to be filled. But suitcases are soon stuffed and distended ... while sponges, ah there, the more you fill them the better they feel. Ha ha! I fixed your wagon for sure that time!

ROGER: Babble on, son of a flyspeck flea-flicker! Nip me, tickle me, give me an irritation! I'm tottering on my sad height! A little more phun and I'll come toppling down to where no starry seat can rescue me! Aborted dreams, no sooner gaining a foothold than torn from the belly, pitched into the trash and half incinerated in the dumping places of general derision producing such dense and odoriferous smoke that you can't as much as open your mouth without your teeth blackening, your tongue growing thick, your constricted words swelling into a cancerous nodule!

BERNARD: Whisper! *(The doorbell rings)* Ough. Ough.

MIMI, *coming in, slipping to the floor, back against the door, totally discouraged*: That damned bitch! ... Ha! ... Ha! ... *(She's not drunk, she's stoned)*

ROGER, *very compassionate, very tender, very sincere. Guitry-eloquent*: What have they done to you this time, my beautiful apparition?

MIMI: Damn their eyes the whole race of them! You try and help them out, that dispossessed race of forsaken forlorners, and they shit on your hands for your troubles! *(She throws her purse to the ground)*

ROGER, *with eager chivalry, picking up her bag*: Who did that, my beautiful emotion, my beautiful commotion?

BERNARD: Who indeed, my beautiful libation? Woof! Woof!

MIMI: You don't know what you're talking about! I didn't have a drop to drink! (...) But I sure had something to smoke! I had to, for them, imagine that, that dispossessed race of thirsty louses! "Just a little puff. Hihihi hahaha, look at her sucking in the fumes!" *(She pushes away Bernard who comes to lick her feet)* You too! Get away from me! I'm not into it! You stump!

BERNARD: Don't you feel well? ...

MIMI: No! I don't feel well for a change! It's not poor little Bernard for once — it's poor little MIMI!

ROGER, *with sobbing voice*: Poor little Mimi.

BERNARD: Woof! Woof!

ROGER: Poor little flame, flicker out. Poor little light forgotten all night in the basement, growing dim behind the dirty screen of the casement window. Poor little demoted votive guttering out in the cold orthodox night of the Oratory ...

> *Mimi is so moved she throws herself on Roger to embrace him. So enthusiastically that he falls over backwards, much to Bernard's delight.*

MIMI, *embarrassed, suddenly straight, leaping up as if on a spring, staring at Roger who is still on the floor, as if he were a large vase she had just broken*: Excuse me. Scuze me. Uhhhh! I didn't do it on purpose, excuse me for living. I-I-I I don't know what got into me ... I'm-I'm-I'm so embarrassed ... Uhhhh! ...

ROGER, *getting up, offended and stiff*: All right already! Don't make it worse!

MIMI, *affirmative*: You're mad! *(Votive)* You're not really mad ... I'm so ashamed! They don't come any more awkward than me! Two left feet! Hayseed! Farmer's daughter! *(Behind her, Bernard mimes winding up her spring)* I always spoil everything! You won't even believe me, but the first time I tried to make love to a guy I peeped all over him ... I was too moved, too spontaneous, it just came out.

I never saw him again. He must have thought I did it on purpose. (...) I bet you think I pushed you over on purpose, right? *(Roger gives an irritated sigh, and Bernard imitates him)* Reassure me, take away my nervousness, tell me you know I didn't push you over on purpose.

ROGER: All right, all right already. All right, all right.

BERNARD: Woof! Woof! ... Woof, woof, already ...

MIMI, *taken by Roger, taking Roger*: It's not all right! Things have never been so bad. My head's spinning and the faster it goes the further I sink. I've started telling my worst secrets without anybody asking me to! *(She turns her anger on Roger, who stands impassively by. She makes him "look the other way" with both hands)* Look the other way at least, you shameless brute, look the other way while I make an ass out of myself! I *am* making an ass out of myself, I know it, they told me enough, those lousy good-for-nothings! I got sick of putting quarters in the jukebox. I told them That's it. They said "What do you mean That's it? You're being an ass again!"

ROGER: Who's "they," my beautiful humiliation?

MIMI, *ah, here's the deluge, she's unchained, unhinged*: All those hhhhhhhores they had there! The minions and munchkins of Queen Sophie the First! They asked me to drive them out to Laval. "Drive us out to Laval, bunghole!" Then one of them absolutely had to drive. "Move over and give me the wheel, bunghole!" I didn't mind but I wanted to make sure she had her license. Hahaha heeheehee, get a load of that one! She hiked up her dress and said, "You want to see my license, here it is, bunghole!" *(Mimi throws her purse as hard as she can across the room, then screams like a madwoman as the lights go down)* Bunghole! Bunghole! Bunghole!

SCENE 4

(Roger, Sophie, Mimi, Bernard)

The police light is lit and flashes in the darkness. Sophie, Mimi and Bernard appear before Roger.

ROGER: You all know why I called you here. To find out who it was. So ... WHO WAS IT? (...) *(No answer)* Instead of doing what you do — and that means you too, Mimi, the further this goes the further you go — instead of drinking and smoking up all my money, I put a little aside. I sacrifice half my savings to save you from bankruptcy, the padlock on the door, your asses on the street, the whole production (...) Well then what do you think happens? To thank me for my trouble you steal the other half. You're all guilty everyone of you because you're all in the same boat — and that means you too, Mimi. But I'd just like to know who actually did it, who stole the coin from under my groin? So ... WHO WAS IT? (...) *(No answer)* I know it wasn't you, Mimi. Tell me it wasn't you.

MIMI, *sobbing*: It wasn't me.

ROGER: I knew it! But her innocence is not so innocent, for it speaks volumes of guilt on the rest of you. So. WHO WAS IT? Was it you, Stump? I saw you stowing two more cases of vodka in the bathroom ... That's 150 dollars' worth and at last count you didn't have a cent.

BERNARD: Mimi lent me the money.

ROGER: She can lend you money for vodka but not to get your glasses fixed? Even though she knows the booze in your blood turns your sight to mud, you might get squished like a pea or fall down and crack open your skull while you're out maneuvering in an alcoholic haze without your ocular prosthesis. Could it be that Mimi wishes you ill? That she's a plotter? How much a plotter is she? Enough to pick the pockets of my Lazy-Boy and throw me into pain and consternation?

BERNARD, *as Mimi sobs harder and harder*: You slime! It's just like you to kick this poor miserable creature who's down on her knees before you as before the Lord Himself! Mimi has money because she sold her car! And you know it! Slime!

ROGER: So Mimi swallowed the bitter pill and sold her Thunderbird so you can go on destroying yourself? I'm edified but that's not the point. So ... Sophie ... WHO WAS IT? Those two are putting themselves in a separate boat and pointing the finger at you ... Are you edified too?

SOPHIE, *leaving, wanting to take the others with her*: Let's go. Come on, everybody! He's on the rag; we'll come back when he comes off it! (...) You too, Mimi! Come on! Don't stay here!

MIMI: I'll stay here if I feel like it. And I feel like it.

> *Sophie and Bernard slam the door on their way out. Lights. Roger is sitting in his armchair. Mimi stands before him. The police flasher has stopped.*

ROGER: You've got circles under your eyes, my beautiful apparition.

MIMI, *wiping her tears as if they were from the 1940s*: I can't sleep. I'm too nervous. I should find a job but I don't know how to do anything and I can't get that off my mind. I wouldn't even be a good whore. A guy would have to be pretty hard up to want someone with two left feet. I'm so glad I can talk to you! Give me guidance: what would you do if you were me?

ROGER, *taking a balled-up piece of paper from his pocket and smoothing it out*: I would ... a solitary bird. Read. Do not be afraid. It doesn't bite, it's Catholic! Taken from the Dichos de Luz y Amor by Saint John of the Cross. A worser poet than me.

MIMI, *reading, taking inspiration along the way*: "A solitary bird must fulfill five conditions. First, fly as high as possible. Then, tolerate no fellow flyers, even those closest to him. Always have his beak pointed heavenward, and have no special color. And last, sing very sweetly."

ROGER: That's good, huh? Tell me how good it is.

MIMI: It's so good it gives me the shivers, it's like a flower in my head, it's like there were voices inside. Voices that encourage me. What I like most is having no special color — you could slip by undetected ... It's like the strange ideas I have ... being with other people, talking to them, touching them, without them even noticing me. Like sitting in your lap when I'm sad and you not even feeling my weight. (...) Do you want to try?

ROGER, *with open arms*: We'll try, my beautiful imagination ... We'll try ... on the condition that you fulfill the fifth criterion of the Dichos de Luz y Amor: that you sing, very sweetly.

MIMI, *sitting on Roger's lap, taking shelter*: I never sing. I don't know any songs. Tell me I'm no heavier than a fly on the ceiling, tell me my breath is no warmer than a cool match in its little box.

ROGER: The melody and the words don't matter; it's the "very sweetly" of it ... *(He hands her another ball of paper)* Sing this.

MIMI, *taking the ball, then springing bolt upright as if she had sat on a tack*: Some other time, okay? I'm too anxious. I have to look after Bernard. If I let Sophie have her way, I'll be spending the rest of my life with a cripple on my hands ...

> She's upset. She goes out and runs straight into Sophie.

MIMI: What did you do with him this time?

SOPHIE, *not in a good mood*: I left him right where he was. I didn't touch him. If he's scratched don't look at my fingernails.

> *Sophie closes the door behind her and stops stock still. She gives Roger a good long look; he collapses abruptly and will spend the ensuing dialogue histry and onyxing, stuttering and shuddering and tail-dragging. Meanwhile, as if from a great distance, we hear Mimi singing, off key and at odd intervals.*

SOPHIE: You didn't pay the light bill, you didn't pay the heating bill, the tenants have formed a union to make faces at us when we go by, Bernard's lost his marbles, the bats in Mimi's belfry are set to spread their wings any minute now, I've started biting my tongue in my sleep, I wake up with a mouthful of blood ... just how far do you want to go?

ROGER: The government broke in and searched the joint. The specspecspec inspectors! They came and spected everything.

SOPHIE, *in babytalk*: They came and spected everything and they left you here? Poor Junior Mints! Oodums poodums. *(Roger sits stone still and cries, wiping his eyes like a child)* Don't cry like that! ... Cry harder, the ones you're crying for can't hear you! *(An unhealthy laugh)* You're suffering too much, Roger. Stop it, you can't go on, it's too mush, I like it too mush! You know me ... A pervert like me's liable to go for your throat and finish you off one last time!

ROGER: Don't bother tearing out my heart; I'll hand it to you on a silver platter.

SOPHIE: Icchh! ... Disgusting! ... Distasteful! ... (...) Don't point that thing at me.

ROGER: Cut the cruelty! If you don't stop I'm going to let myself go, I'll fall down, I'll roll around on the floor, I'll scream. *(Lying down on the floor)* Why don't you lie down with me?

SOPHIE: You want tenderness now? Is that it?

ROGER: That's right! That's it! Tenderness! Quick! Just a drop! I'm burning for it!

SOPHIE, *lowering herself*: What's this tenderness thing all about? ... I've heard a lot about it but I've never seen any. Is it something like this? *(She spits in his face)*

ROGER: That's right! That's it! The nail on the head! Encore! Encore! Gimmee summore! Summore summore! Quick! If you don't gimmee summore right away, I'm warning you! I'm warning you!

SOPHIE: Warn me again and see what happens!

ROGER, *louder*: I'm warning you!

SOPHIE, *threatening*: I'm giving you one more warning and that's all you'll get. I'm warning you: if you warn me again I'll bite you!

ROGER, *getting up, running away*: I'm warning you! I'm warning you! I'm warning you!

SOPHIE, *catching Roger, jumping on his back and biting into the collar of his bathrobe*: I warned you! When I bite, I get my pound of flesh.

ROGER, *yelling and running like a madman with Sophie on his back*: Help! S.O.S.! Enough! Oh! Stop! Tetanus! Botulism!

MIMI, *we hear her cries before we see her*: Roger! ... Roger! *(She comes in)* Roger! *(She stops in her tracks, amazed by the equestrian scene before her. Then she rushes to Roger's rescue)* Let go of him! *(She hits Sophie with her purse)* Let go of him! Roger! Help me! Bernard can't stand up any more! He's falling on his face! And he's not even drunk! *(Hits Sophie again)* Let go of him!

SOPHIE: Mimi! Let go of me! I'm warning you!

MIMI, *hitting her again*: Let go of him!

SOPHIE, *she lets go of Roger, falls on all fours and begins chasing Mimi*: Roger! Roger!

ROGER, *taking off his bathrobe, totally absorbed in inspecting his collar*: Oodums. Poodums. Now what, you harping carping harpy whores? Oodums. Oodums poodums oodums poodums. Poodums poodums oodums poodums! Now what?

BERNARD, *appearing in the doorway, staggering, falling backwards down the stairway*: Whisper ...

SOPHIE, *calling off her Mimi-hunt to rescue Bernard*: Great! Great!

MIMI, *pushing Roger to the floor by nestling against him too violently to find shelter*: Great! *(Shaking her head, hands covering her face, ashamed)* Great!

SCENE 5

```
┌─────────────────────────────────────────┐
│ _____                  _____ │
│                                          │
└─────────────────────────────────────────┘
```

(Mimi, Roger)

Blackout. Mimi and Roger begin their dialogue on the stairs. They are carrying something like an eviscerated throne that will replace the single chair set before the banquet. Mimi is panicky, out of breath; Roger is calm and precise.

MIMI'S VOICE: Give me strength. I feel like it was all my fault, like I pushed him. You're my best friend, help me.

ROGER'S VOICE: Repeat your Brittle Speech and hold your nose. Do what I do.

MIMI'S VOICE, *obeying*: "The stump toppled down the stairs. I will go further, I will go as far as to say that he plunged, he took a hell of a fall down the narrow hall."

ROGER'S VOICE: Ananan ommrill gadferim: he chose what he wanted and he got what he chose.

MIMI'S VOICE: "Ananan ommreel ..."

ROGER'S VOICE, *stopping her*: No! Ananan ommrill! A shade of meaning!

MIMI'S VOICE: "Ommrill gadferim: he chose what he deserved ..." Did I get it?

ROGER'S VOICE: Not quite but it's just as well. Don't let's stop: I have a choice too and the sordid tribulations of a stump are not of my choosing.

MIMI'S VOICE: "I have a choice too and the sordid tribulations of a stump are not of my choosing!"

ROGER'S VOICE: Hurray!

MIMI'S VOICE: Hurray!

ROGER'S VOICE: Again, my bold beauty. Again again!

MIMI'S VOICE, *they enter the room, though still in the dark*: I have a choice too, hurray! hurray! hurray! (...) Do you really think it's going to be okay? Do you think I'm really equipped to vault over Bernard and not fall and drag my anchor? Say yes!

ROGER'S VOICE: When you speak the name of the trap, when you designate it, you're not trapped any more — the trap is.

MIMI'S VOICE, *enthusiastically*: You're so encouraging!

ROGER'S VOICE: Nothing to it. You tune your one-track onto one thing: being encouraged by me.

> *Lights. They push the chair out of the way and replace it with the throne.*

MIMI: It *is* one-track, so be careful ... I turn turbulent. I'm too sensitive, even to encouragement. I'm still sweating, my forehead is all tight. Be careful ... I wear your words like a crown. I look at myself in the mirror when you speak to me and I grow beautiful with everything you put into my mind. Be careful for yourself ... When I latch onto someone I'm a leach, a stubborn stain ...

ROGER, *slapping the dusty seat of the throne, pulling on the protruding springs*: That's just the thing for what Lucie's got.

MIMI: What does she have?

ROGER: A derriere.

MIMI, *laughing, bent double*: I know you're serious, I don't know why I'm laughing so much ...

ROGER, *holding his nose to quote Nelligan*: You laugh like in: "Oh, so joyful I fear that I fear that I fear ... I will burst into tears."

MIMI, *voluble*: You understand everything ... I feel ... exposed, like a slug when you turn over a stone in the field behind your house. Did you ever do that, turn over stones in the field behind your house to see the strange little bugs with all their wriggling feet that live underneath? ... You had to be quick, right? They disappeared down their little tunnels so fast! I'm so afraid for Bernard ... afraid he'll die — and everyone will think it was my fault. Poor Bernard ... I turned him into an alcoholic, I made him impotent, I didn't take care of him like I should have. Poor Bernard ... He was counting so much on me to save him!

ROGER, *taking Mimi by the waist and seating her none too gently on the throne, then sitting at her feet*: Before wanting-to-be-saved there's wanting-to-be-unsalvageable. Yes, such things happen, child! Yes they do! They do! *(Getting impatient)* Yes and if you keep on waving Bernard in my face, I'm warning you, I'm warning you, I'm dropping my ruck, I'm fleecing I'm creasing I'm freezing the puck! Are you comfortable?

MIMI: Not really no but I can't tell the difference, I'm too nervous, all I want to do is talk, let me talk, if you don't want me to talk about Bernard I'll tell you about the dream I had last night. I'll tell you about it, okay? It'll do me good to talk about it, don't you think?

ROGER, *who throughout Mimi's story will tear the lower part of her long dress into ever narrowing longitudinal strips.* Well well, so Bernard's accident's not what's bothering you, it's that swollen tongue of yours ...

MIMI: You drip! ... *(Embarrassed by Roger's efforts but afraid to do anything about it)* Why are you doing that? You're embarrassing me ... I'm not wearing nylons ... (...) Do you want me to tell you my dream, yes or no? *(Roger is too absorbed in his work)* I'm going to tell you anyway, Mr. Stoop! There were lots of people, like at Dorval over the holidays. But nobody was there for anybody else, nobody was waiting for a plane. Everybody was keeping to himself, we were stretching our legs, we were getting a little impatient. We were careful not to get in each other's way but there were too many of us not to run into each other once in a while. The important thing was to do your best, and since everyone understood no one got mad at anyone else. (...) You understand? *(Embarrassed by Roger's work, she crosses her legs)* Are you listening to me or not?

ROGER, *uncrossing her legs, she doesn't resist*: I'll listen to you if you sit still. If you try to slip away I will too.

MIMI: I'm ready to be led, but don't shunt me around so much, don't whip me back and forth from side to side every which way. You just got through saying, "Choose, decide what you want." Well, I decided to cross my legs but you go and uncross them for me, then you tell me to let myself go ...

ROGER: Are you an insect, some sort of scolopendra, just for fun — or for real? Do scolopendra or millipedes cross their legs?

MIMI, *she's decided to let herself go*: If I let myself go, I suffer. If I don't let myself go, I feel guilty. If that's what it means to choose, I might as well go back to my dream ... At first, everyone was polite. When we brushed up against each other, we nodded, we smiled, we said excuse-me-sorry-it-was-an-accident ... Then suddenly everything changed. Not that anything actually happened, but we saw that everyone who'd gotten touched had slashes in their clothes, burning wounds that got infected and stank. Then we heard on the loudspeaker that there was an epidemic. Everyone believed it, everyone went running for the exits. We all wanted to get out, we fought, we shoved, we pushed each other out of the way. It was horrible. Because the more we jammed together, the more slashes and wounds we got, the weakest and strongest alike. Then they started yelling, Stop-stop-it's-not-the-end-of-the-world-it's-just-a-game-of-tag. But it was too late. I looked at myself, I was all rotting away. (...) *(She shakes Roger)* What do you think that means?

ROGER: What's tag?

MIMI, *surprised*: You don't know about tag-you're-it-you've-got-hydrophobia? (...) You never played tag when you were little? (...) I can't believe it! *(She jumps to her feet and goes and hides behind the sofa)* Quick, run away! I'll count to three! One two three! ... *(She leaps up and touches Roger with her hand)* Tag you're it! *(She hides behind the sofa again)* I tagged you, you're it! You're it! You have to catch me and tag me now.

ROGER: If I don't?

MIMI, *she moves closer to him, challenging him, playful but febrile*: If you don't … If you don't … *(She doesn't know what to say)* I won't tell you! You'll find out soon enough …

ROGER, *he takes the chair that was replaced by the throne and walks out with it*: If that's the way it is, I'd rather keep the tag … Ha ha!

MIMI, *following Roger, helping him carry the chair, helping him open the door, wanting so much to help him*: Wait, I'll go with you, I can help you.

> *They carry the chair down to a storeroom at the end of the hall. We hear their dialogue as they come and go.*

MIMI'S VOICE: I've got a present for you. I wanted to give it to you but after what happened …

ROGER'S VOICE, *angry*: What happened? Go ahead! I dare you! Name it! Designate it! Spit it out! (…) (…) You mean after Zapotek was spurred into a sprint in the paddock … Pereat Pete, pereat Pete!

MIMI'S VOICE, *submissive*: "After Zakopet was spurned into a snit over the haddock."

ROGER'S VOICE, *pulling the reins*: Zatopek! Zatopek! Zatopek because that stump ran himself to ruin by dethroning all the records! Not haddock! Paddock! Paddock committee because none of you can get organized! (…)

MIMI'S VOICE: You get so upset. I promise I won't ever talk about him again.

ROGER'S VOICE: Him who? You mean the Stump? Why don't you say the Stump?

MIMI'S VOICE: I've said it enough.

ROGER'S VOICE: You haven't said it enough if it still means something to you when I say it! Oodums! Oodums poodums! Oodums poodums poodums oodums poodums! (…) (…) (…)

> *A cry issues from Mimi; Roger has touched her somewhere.*

82

MIMI'S VOICE, *she's wounded, but turns it into a game*: Ouch! (...) You touched me so you're it now, ha ha, you've got hydrophobia!

> *She runs away.*

ROGER'S VOICE: I touched you but I didn't say you're it, it doesn't count, ha ha!

MIMI'S VOICE: We're having lots of phun ... but it hurts me ... the way you take my affection for you ...

ROGER'S VOICE: With my hands? ...

MIMI'S VOICE: With your hands ... You don't always do it that way of course. There's other things between us ... (...) (...) (...) I'm — I'm a Lesbian. (...) Sophie made me take a test the other day. She said kiss me on the mouth like a man and if that does something for you you're a Lesbian. (...) Then ... then she wouldn't let go of me ... what it did was make me want to vomit ... (...) Don't tell Sophie I told you, okay? Okay?

> *They go back inside the apartment. Roger sits down in his Lazy-Boy. Mimi paces in circles, more nervous than ever.*

MIMI: I left the phone number. Why hasn't the hospital called?

ROGER: Because Bell Telephone cut off the telephone. *(He opens his arms to her, employing his Guitryloquent voice)* Come sit down on my lap, kit-kat.

MIMI, *gently but firmly*: No.

ROGER: Come place your negligible weight upon me.

MIMI, *sad*: No.

ROGER: Come ...

MIMI, *sadder*: No. *(She remembers her present and seizes the opportunity)* Don't you want to see what I got you? Wait! *(Running to her room, appearing a moment later with her purse)* You'll be surprised, you'll be happy, you'll be insecure. *(She pulls a bundle of bills from her bag)* Look! $3,000 ... It's not $5,000, I know ... *(She ventures closer to him, offering the money)* Don't be afraid, take it, I can't do anything with it anyway. Take it ... do it for me ... it's no sacrifice ... I cashed in part of a pension plan ...

ROGER: Don't talk so loud ... shhhhhh. *(He steers Mimi toward the table and hides under it with her)* Hide it ... shhh ... hide it quick. Don't show it to them, never show them that kind of thing ... Listen, dum-dum, let me tell you about treasures. You have to have a treasure, dum-dum, a secret, a ransom. Do like I do: no one stole my last $5,000, that was a lie. I made it up and put on the trial just so they'd think I'd lost my ransom. Understand? You can't trust them. Shhhhh ... Hide everything that matters to them, give them what they give you: all manner of false gifts. They'll give you body and soul, but what do they care about their bodies and their souls, you tell me that! They use them to make monkeys out of us so we'll think they get paid in peanuts! Shhhhhhhhhhh ... hide that real money!

MIMI: What good is a ransom?

ROGER: With a good ransom you'll never get caught, you'll never get stuck inside where you can't get out.

MIMI, *stuffing the money into one of Roger's pockets*: Take my ransom, I don't have any place to go anyway.

ROGER, *she tries to get up, he holds her back, takes her hand, strokes it*: We're not talking some little treasure that'll get you an airplane ticket — with this you can buy the whole airport.

MIMI, *her anguish and horror at being touched join hands*: You want my hand? Take it. Take my elbow! Take my shoulder! Take it! And leave! Go away! *(She tries to get up but he holds her back)* What will it take to get you to go?

ROGER: A kiss.

MIMI, *kissing him hard and fast on the mouth*: All right?

ROGER: No. I want a kiss like the last time.

MIMI, *sighing, kissing again*: Like that?

ROGER, *pitiless*: I said like last time!

MIMI, *full of good will despite everything*: What last time?

ROGER: The time you whispered hmmmm it's good. Hmmmm it's good, oodums poodums. Don't go and tell me you don't remember!

MIMI, *trying again, with a show of conviction*: Hmmmmmmmm it's gooooood (...) All right? (...) Are you free now? Can you go now?

ROGER, *stubbornly*: It was for real last time!

MIMI: I don't remember how I kissed you, not that time, not any time. I forgot every single kiss! And quick too! ... The only thing I remember is that every time we start in it turns sour, and it's going to turn sour this time too.

ROGER: Not true! The time I'm talking about was sweet. Try again, abandon yourself harder. When you get it right, I'll go Shhhhhh, then you'll understand, dum-dum, what shhhh means.

MIMI, *kissing Roger again, practically at the end of her rope*: Hmmmmmmmm that's good.

ROGER: Goo it summore. Goo it summore encore!

MIMI: Hmmmmmmmmmmm that's good!

> *The lights dim.*

ROGER: Summore summore!

MIMI: Hmmmmmmmm that's good! Good good good!

ROGER: One more time. Then that'll be it.

MIMI, *crying*: I can't do it any more!

ROGER: Once more into the breach! If you don't, I'm warning you, it's going to turn sour again.

MIMI: Hmm that's good! Ah it's good! Ah it's awful good! Hmm!

The lights are completely down.

ROGER: Shhhhhhhhhhh ... (...) Repeat after me! Respond already, dum-dum!

MIMI: Shhhhhhhhhhh ...

SCENE 6

(Sophie, Roger, Mimi, Bernard)

Black-out. Roger and Mimi's shushes tail off. Then we hear the forced laughter of the surprise party. Lights. The four characters are holding bottles and they've had more than their share. Roger, the most gleeful of the bunch, is leading Sophie across the room in a kind of primate tango. Bernard has put on Roger's smoking jacket and is actually sitting in the Lazy-Boy! He wears an orthopedic collar. Haggard, Mimi takes a few steps.

ROGER, *falling exhausted under Sophie, who pulls of his shoes and throws them away*: Ha! ... Ha! When we have phun don't we have a ton, we've got phun on the run, hey hon hey hon!

SOPHIE, *getting to her feet quickly*: It's some phun, but it's not enough. Lucie told me straight out: if we don't have any more phun than this, if we don't have some really big phun, if we don't die laughing, if we don't bust a gut — she won't come!

MIMI: If she doesn't come, how's she going to know whether or not we're having more phun than we can stand?

> *That's a good one! Roger throws himself into Sophie's arms, better to laugh. Seeing this, Mimi throws herself into Bernard's, with all the respect due his orthopedic collar. She laughs better too.*

BERNARD: Hey, guys ... should we tell her?

SOPHIE AND ROGER: Go ahead, go on and tell her!

BERNARD: Uhh ... Mimi ... my effeminine better half ... *(Phun must be had at all costs. At the slightest hint of a joke, everybody laughs heartily)* Uhh ... Mimi ... my beloved ex-heartstone ... because I don't know if you know but you're burning another log in there now ... You told Roger that all hells being equal you'd rather stoke his fire than mine. Don't tell me different, Roger told me himself. Ask Roger! He's right there, ask him! Right, guys? Right? Right? Anyway ... Mimi ... my beloved strife ... there's something I've been meaning to express myself to you, and that's that you might as well stop waiting for Lucie. There aren't any more Lucies! There used to be, but not any more, the pigs ate them all up ... Right, boys? Right?

SOPHIE AND ROGER: That's right! That's right for sure!

MIMI, *putting down her bottle, then setting about to rip her dress, throwing herself at Sophie who offers no resistance, she's laughing too hard, tearing her dress too*: Well how about that! That's just great! Great! The whole time you knew Lucie wasn't coming ... And you let me go rushing around looking for fabrics and drawing patterns! You knew it and you let me get all nervous and excited, I spent all week with a thimble on my thumb so I'd be chic and not make you ashamed! Well how about that! That's just great! Great!

BERNARD, *more and more pompously*: It's not just the Lucies, Mimi! It's the Bernards too! There used to be heaps of them in the old days! How many did you take? You wouldn't have served yourself too generously, would you have? There hasn't been a quarter of a single one ... not a third ... not even a half!

MIMI, *retaking possession of her bottle*: I took some? I served myself too generously! Me? Me?

BERNARD: Right, you! You! No use denying, no use being stubborn, no one'll tell you different. There's nobody here except you. Right, you guys?

SOPHIE AND ROGER, *calling with ghostly voices*: Mimiiii! Mimiiiiiiii!

MIMI: Yeeeeeees!

BERNARD: See, you're here. You recognized yourself right off and you answered. (...) Call Lucie if you don't believe me! *(Mimi does not call; she drinks)* She's too shy. We'll call her ourselves.

BERNARD, SOPHIE AND ROGER: Lucie! Luuuuuuuucie! Luciiiiiie!

88

BERNARD: See: no Lucie! Do you see a Lucie? Do you see a little motor to run my pup's tail? I shouldn't talk about my dog: my dog is dead. Why don't you call Bernard instead? You're not shy with Bernard — call him! You never know there might be a little scrap left, a crumb ... Not to mention a quarter of an oodums of a half of a poodums of one. Not that I want to use the favorite expression of a certain canker sore I know that I could name but prefer not to.

> *Sophie and Roger join Bernard, better to laugh and congratulate each other for all the phun they're having. Mimi sinks to the floor to sulk. And that breaks their hearts. And they fly to her rescue, very proselytical.*

SOPHIE, ROGER AND BERNARD, *not in unison*: Okay! ... Okay! ... Okay! ... Okay! ... Okay! ...

> *They kneel around Mimi and caress her none too tenderly.*

SOPHIE: Itty bitty teeny weeny Mimi crumbcake ... listen up! All of us here, even Roger, we're all doing the best we can. Stand up on your own two feet like we do, make an effort, laugh a little. We're having a surprise party, it's time to unfurl our tentacles and hold on tight. If one of us lets go ... no more party ... all fall down!

ROGER, *begging Mimi*: Oodums poodums! Oodums poodums poodums! Poodums oodums oodums!

BERNARD: Mimi, the Master has spoken. The Master has said "Oodums poodums! Oodums poodums poodums! Poodums oodums oodums!"

MIMI, *getting up, pushing everyone away furiously*: Don't touch me! *(The upraised bottle empties onto her head ... and threatens to knock out whoever would dare touch her again)* Don't! Touch! Me!

SOPHIE, *caressingly*: Not even me! *(Tragically)* Your best friend?

MIMI, *screaming*: Just try it! ... Come on! Try it!

SOPHIE, *braving Mimi, getting closer with outstretched hands, talking babytalk*: Baby no have to worry, Roger it, not me. I not it. I no have hydrophobia. (*She makes a fat kissing noise in Mimi's direction*) Don't be nasty-nasty, oodums poodums poodums oodums ... (*Mimi slaps one of Sophie's hands*)

ROGER AND BERNARD, *while Sophie goes running every which way at once, whimpering, staggering, as if dealt a mortal blow*: Ha ha! ... Ha ha! ... Ha ha! ...

MIMI: You've put your hands all over me! You've stuck them into my heart! You've crammed them into my head! You can't lift a finger without grinding your filth into my pores! You can't say a word without injecting infection into my feelings and fondest notions! You're a bunch of ... (*She takes a hit of vodka*) slop-slingers, a bunch of slutch-clutch-ers ... a bunch of shithouse tippers!

ROGER, *hierarchical*: Agnus Dei qui tollis peccata mundi ...

BERNARD AND SOPHIE, *getting down to kneel*: Oremus ... bray for us!

MIMI, *turning on her heels, tapping one, clacking the other*: I quit! I don't want to hear another word out of you! I know those peepncreep shows of yours! You suckered me in all right ... non-stop, and I bit the bait, I was afraid to stand up to my height, always on all fours, on two knees, I let myself be had ... I didn't know where I was any more ... or who I was with ... Enough's enough! Now you're going to shut your traps and I'm going to put on the show!

ROGER, *calling for silence, then heading for his tape recorder*: Shhhhhhhhhhh ...

SOPHIE AND BERNARD, *billing and cooing through the recorded drum rolls that finish in a crash of cymbals, then booing Mimi*: Booooooooooo! ... Boo!

MIMI, *to Roger*: Aren't you booing the home team too? Oodums! Oodums poodums!

ROGER: Me boo with the hoos? Me? Me boo you who took an hour to give me a good kiss after all I taught you? ... (*Then booing her louder than the others*) Boooooooooooo!

MIMI, *everyone pulling on his individual bottle, and Mimi more individually than the others*: Go ahead, everybody! Talk Chinese so I won't understand. Dance me into a corner and say, "Glisten up! Glisten up, heartache, I've got nothing to tell you and I'm not going to say what it is, I rather keep it to myself!" Make yourselves scarce! Tell me, "Take me! Take me so I can show you how well I wriggle loose!"

SOPHIE: Now that's the limit! Christ on a crutch! Quick on the bellyache, aren't you, Miss Goody Two-Shoes! As soon as we let go of you you're complaining how we've stopped caring! Christ on a bike!

BERNARD, *sitting back down in the Lazy-Boy and putting on airs*: Wow now! She took a haymaker to the heart, art! ...

MIMI, *beginning to stagger*: Shut up, you! Shut it up tight! That's right, you! *(Grabbing the bottle and emptying it in his face)* Shut up and tipple! Drink, you fish! You're through scaring me with it! You're through driving me out of my mind! It doesn't do a thing to me now! Drink! Wet your whistle! You're cute when you drink! *(The bottle is empty)* Too sad! You ran out! Poor teddybear! *(Swinging around, dashing into the bathroom to get another case)* Stand by! Temporary technical difficulties! Do not adjust your set!

BERNARD, *to Sophie and Roger, who've lain down on the sofa exhausted, holding each other in their arms like a pair of turtledoves*: She's getting tipsy all right ... she's oozing her ibinitions!

ROGER: Now this is phun!

SOPHIE, *as Mimi comes out of the bathroom with the case*: Curb your bitch. She's got the rabies, she might bite somebody.

MIMI, *scandalized by Sophie and Roger's billing and cooing, she stops, screams, drops the case on the table, glasses, plates, meats and wines go flying, she runs into the bathroom, slams the door, howls*: Now they've started loving each other! They're squirming and clutching! They're chucking each other under the chin! Now that's phun!

SOPHIE, *to Bernard*: What'd I tell you? I'm warning you: scoop your poop before it's too late!

MIMI, *shooting out of the bathroom, going to fish two bottles from the case, issuing a challenge to Bernard*: And you-you ...you-you ... I've had it with you bragging about how no one can match you drink for drink. Here! *(She gives him a bottle, opens the other for herself)* I'll match you! I'll bet you anything I'll finish my bottle before you ... *(She hiccups)* before yours!

BERNARD, *taking the whole thing ab ovo*: Don't bother, I'm going to lose, I like losing too much! It's like my eyes ... Doctor Wormwood told me I'm not losing my sight cause of my drinking — I was just born to lose, I've got it in the blood. Doc said to me, "Bernie, you've blown your life, okay! ... That's a real piece of work. But that's not the half of it: you're going to blow your death too." *(He hoots and snorts)* He told me, "You're just a stranger to success. And you want to die so much, I wouldn't be surprised if you blow that too ... you won't ever die!" *(Another burst of laughter)*

MIMI, *still spoiling for a bet, as Sophie and Roger take care of their business ... with growing tenderness*: Cmon! What do you bet?

BERNARD: I'll bet what you bet ... if you've got anything to bet.

MIMI: I'll bet all the love I once had for you.

BERNARD: A loser like me usually likes dropping more than that. I rather wager away a quarter than what's between us.

MIMI: You're not just any kitchen garden buffoon! You're a grrrrrrreat clown! In the acrobatic style! We scream, we cry, we're afraid you'll break your neck ... but you always land on your feet. *(She ingests another drink)* All right, I'll make a deal with you: I bet you a fall down the stairs ... That way we'll both come out on the bottom ... I'll spurn a sprint like Zakopet in the paddock ... and you'll lose yor wager ...

BERNARD, *singing*: A woman's heart is a flighty thing. *(He drinks)* You can capture it once, but it'll never sing.

MIMI, *turning and jostling Roger and Sophie who are cooing like pigeons under the eaves, then taking a run at Bernard and crosscheck-ing him*: Great! ... Great! ... Nobody wants to watch my show!

Some of them're ... kissing ... licking each other like newborn calves ... one of whom among them's already licked my halves ... Those somes're going *(imitating Sophie and Roger's sighs)* ahhh-haaa-hummm-ummm ... while the other one *(à propos of Bernard)* doesn't think I'm a good enough artress, arktruss, actriste ... to mount the boards! I don't care! I don't care! I'm going to do my show anyway.

> *She hiccups and resolves to climb onto the table with her bottle.*

BERNARD, *fooling with the tape recorder to play the drum-rolls and cymbal-crashing tape*: Do it anyway, sweetheart honeybunch. Don't care, do it anyway! But wait a minute, you're all naked up there, wait, I'm going to give you an introduction.

MIMI, *climbing onto the table, kicking away the rest of the banquet ... while the lights go down except a single spot on her, as Bernard's introduction is finally heard*: Ladies and Gentlemen ... Cows and Bulls ... I have gathered here tonight to give you an original interpretation of my imitation — oops sorry scuze me for living — my intimidation routine! *(With bottle heavenward)* Okay now watch out: I'm going to do it ... Shhhhhhhhhh ... Watch me! Don't avert your eyes! Hold onto your hats! Be witness to the feat!

> *Mimi raises the bottle to her lips as the drum rolls begin. She drinks and drinks, the lights dim and dim, the drum rolls and rolls.*
> *Mimi staggers, Mimi is going to collapse, the lights go out, the cymbal crash is heard: immediately after the lights begin to come up.*
> *Mimi is lying on the table. Sophie, Roger and Bernard appear from the rear of the apartment, moving forward, dressed in Santa Claus suits, as Sophie and Roger were in the last scene of Part One.*
> *Mimi sees them, screams, howls, gets to her feet, jumps off the table, runs.*

MIMI, *not like Goody Two-Shoes this time, more like a child beseiged by monsters*: Don't touch me! Don't touch me! Don't touch me!

SOPHIE, BERNARD AND ROGER, *running after Mimi and touching her as much and as often as they can, like they were playing tag, but we hear children's voices instead of theirs*: You're it! It doesn't count I wasn't it! Ha ha! ... You're it! You've got hydrophobia! I tagged you but I wasn't really it, HA HA! *(The "Introduction" tape begins to play)* I tagged you but I didn't say you're it! Ha ha! ... Hydrophobia! It doesn't count! It doesn't count ... Ha ha! ...

> *Hysterical, oniric, blinded, deafened, face undone, Mimi runs to the edge of the stage, where her undone face is visible to all, including herself.*
> *Mimi is lost. She hestitates. She is going to jump from the stage. She jumps ... just as the cymbals clash once more, the lights go down, and Roger's semaphoric system — red flasher and siren — goes into motion ... and as a chorus of children's voices sings out in unison ...*

YOU'RE IT!